JAPANESE WORDS
& THEIR USES

JAPANESE WORDS & THEIR USES

Volume II

by Akira Miura

TUTTLE PUBLISHING

Rutland • Boston • Tokyo

First published in 2002 by Tuttle Publishing, an imprint of Periplus Editions (HK) Ltd., with editorial offices at 153 Milk Street, Boston, Massachusetts 02109.

LC Card No. 82-51099
ISBN 0-8048-3249-8

Distributed by

USA
Tuttle Publishing
Distribution Center
Airport Industrial Park
364 Innovation Drive
North Clarendon, VT 05759-9436
Tel: (800) 526-2778
Tel: (802) 773-8930
Fax: (800) 329-8885

JAPAN
Tuttle Publishing
RK building, 2nd Floor
2-13-10 Shimo-Meguro
Meguro-ku
Tokyo 153 0064
Tel: 81-35-437-0171
Fax: 81-35-437-0755

SOUTHEAST ASIA
Berkeley Books Pte. Ltd.
130 Joo Seng Road
#06-01/03 Olivine Building
Singapore 368357
Tel: (65) 280-1330
Fax: (65) 280-6290

First edition
06 05 04 03 02 01 00 99   10 9 8 7 6 5 4 3 2 1

Printed in the United States of America

TABLE OF CONTENTS

PREFACE

I have been teaching Japanese to Americans for more than 35 years. During that time I have observed a large number of errors in Japanese made by my American students. Most of those errors are due to the students' insufficient mastery of Japanese grammar (for example, their inability to inflect verbs correctly or to use appropriate particles), but there are also at least as many errors that are basically attributable to vocabulary problems.

When the American student of Japanese first comes across a new Japanese word, it is usually introduced with an English translation, which is considered the "equivalent," e.g., *atatakai* is matched up with "warm." The student is therefore very likely to conclude that there is in fact a one-to-one correspondence between the two words, and he/she does indeed start using *atatakai,* for example, in all situations where warm would be called for in English. He/She might thus say to a Japanese friend in the middle of summer, with the mercury hitting the mid-80s Fahrenheit, *Kyoo wa atatakai desu nee* "It's warm today, isn't it!" That would really baffle the poor Japanese friend because, in Japanese, temperatures that high are not *atatakai,* but *atsui* "hot." *Atatakai* most aptly describes a nice spring day that arrives after the cold months of winter.

The first volume of *Japanese Words and Their Uses* (1983) [herafter referred to as *JWTU1*] was thus born out of my concern about American students' difficulty with Japanese vocabulary. The book was fortunately very warmly received. The only problem was that it handled only about 300 basic words, which of course was not enough for students as they progressed to higher levels. Because I realized that, I started collecting more samples of student errors, and when I felt I had enough samples, I decided to write a sequel to *JWTU1*. It took me almost three years to write this new volume. As in the case of the first volume, I explained not only how a particular word should be used, but also how it should not be. Whenever possible, I contrasted Japanese words with their English counterparts. Many of the errors cited in this volume were actually committed by my own students (although they were not always quoted verbatim).

There are just as many synonyms in Japanese as there are in English, and they create problems for students of Japanese. For example, both *binboo* and *mazushii* mean "poor," but they differ in usage. In this book, I included a number of synonyms like that with sample sentences as well as explanations of their differences.

A significant difference between the first volume and the second one is that the latter uses more Japanese script. The reason is that I feel students who read this sequel are probably more advanced than those who used the original one, and are therefore not only more capable of handling the script but will probably benefit more from it.

I would like to express my appreciation to the Australian National University, which gave me a research grant for two months in 1996, thus enabling me to begin writing the manuscript. Thanks are also due to my wife, Charlotte, who proofread the final draft for me.

—AKIRA MIURA

EXPLANATORY NOTES

ARRANGEMENT OF ENTRIES

The main text of this book consists of a list of about 250 Japanese terms. Each entry heading gives the term in romanization, and in Japanese kanji (ideographic characters) and/or *kana* (syllabics), then one or more English "equivalents." The kanji usage is limited to those widely in use. The heading is then followed by a detailed explanation of the term's usage.

TERMINOLOGY

Since this book is meant not as a scholarly treatise but rather as a reference book for elementary- through intermediate-level students, the number of technical terms has been kept to a minimum.

   ***I*-Adjectives.** They are inflected words that end in *-ai, -ii, -ui,* or *-oi. Hayai* "fast," *ookii* "large," *furui* "old," and *hiroi* "wide," for example, are *i*-adjectives.

Na-**Adjectives.** *Na*-adjectives are so called because when they are used to modify a noun, they require *na,* as in *kirei na hana* "a beautiful flower" or *iya na hito* "a nasty person." *Na*-adjectives may sometimes be called *na*-nouns by other authors. Other examples of *na*-adjectives are *genki* "healthy" and *shitsurei* "rude."

Particles. Japanese particles are uninflected words that occur within or at the end of a sentence. They generally do not begin an utterance. When they occur within a sentence, they relate what precedes (whether a word, a phrase, or a clause) to what follows. (For this reason, particles are sometimes called "relationals.") Examples of this type are *wa, ga, o,* and *to.* Particles that occur at the end of a sentence are called sentence-final particles, and they make the sentence interrogative, exclamatory, emphatic, etc. Examples of this type are *ka, nee,* and *yo.*

Potential forms of verbs. Potential forms are forms that mean "can do such and such" or "such and such can be done." *Yomeru,* for example, is the potential form of *yomu* "to read" and means "can read" or "can be read."

Punctual verbs. Verbs representing actions or occurrences that take place without duration over time are punctual verbs. *Shinu* "to die," *tsuku* "to arrive" and *kekkon-suru* "to get married" are examples of this type.

Stative verbs. Verbs that express states rather than actions are stative verbs. *Iru* "(someone) is (somewhere)" and *aru* "(something) is (somewhere)" are examples of this category.

JAPANESE ACCENT

Accent marks are used in this book. They are, as a rule, used in the entry headings only, e.g., o͞okī͞.

Unlike English, which has a stress accent, Japanese has a pitch accent. In Japanese words, each syllable is spoken either high or low. If the first syllable is low, the second is always high, and if the first syllable is high, the second is always low. In this book, the mark ⌐ indicates a rise in pitch, and the mark ¬ indicates a fall in pitch. The syllable followed by ¬ is always the accented syllable. For example, OOKII, a four-syllable word, should be pronounced low-high-high-low, and KI, the last syllable before the fall, is the accented syllable. Some words are left completely unmarked, e.g., KIMONO. Unmarked words are accentless (or unaccented) words, i.e., words that do not have a fall in pitch. In accentless words, the first syllable is always low, but the remaining syllables are all high, and there is no fall in pitch even when the words are followed by a particle. For example, *kimono wa* is pronounced:

$$ki^{mono\ wa}$$

Words that end with an accented syllable (e.g., ATAMA) have the same accent pattern as accentless words when pronounced by themselves, but when they are followed by a particle, a difference emerges. For example, ATAMA (accented) and KIMONO (accentless) have exactly the same pitch pattern when pronounced alone, but when followed by a particle (e.g., *wa*) they are pronounced differently, as follows:

$$atama\ wa \rightarrow a^{tama}\ wa$$

$$kimono\ wa \rightarrow ki^{mono\ wa}$$

Note that *wa* in *atama wa* is low while *wa* in *kimono wa* is high.

ROMANIZATION

The system of romanization used in this book is the popular Hepburn system. There are, however, some differences that should be mentioned. In this book, ん is always written *n*, even before *m, p,* and *b*. When *n* should be pronounced independently of a vowel or y that follows it, an apostrophe is inserted to indicate the fact. Long vowels are generally shown by doubling the vowels (e.g., *aa* and *oo*) instead of by using macrons. Long vowels, however, are not indicated in the proper names that appear in the bibliography.

OTHER CONVENTIONS

An asterisk is used in this book to mark incorrect utterances. A question mark at the beginning of a sentence indicates unnaturalness or awkwardness.

JAPANESE WORDS AND THEIR USES

ABIRU 浴びる to take a bath, shower

Japanese people who have spent a number of years in English-speaking countries such as the United States often end up having their spoken Japanese affected by English. One example of that I once heard from such a Japanese was *Moo shawaa o torimashita ka,* a direct translation of "Have you taken a shower yet?" In authentic Japanese, the sentence should be *Shawaa o abimashita ka,* using the verb *abiru* rather than *toru.*

"Take a bath" also can be *furo o abiru,* although another expression *furo ni hairu* is probably more common.

1. 日本人は風呂を浴びる (or 風呂に入る)のが本当に好き
   だ。
   Nihonjin wa furo o abiru (or furo ni hairu) no ga hontoo ni suki da.
   The Japanese really love taking baths.

ACHIKOCHI あちこち here and there

あちこち, short for あちらこちら, looks very much like English "here and there," except that the order is reversed, i.e., あちこち literally would be "there and here." Although あちこち and "here and there" are quite similar in meaning, there is a slight difference. あちこち seems to cover a wider area than "here and there," as in the following example.

1. あちこち捜したけれど見つからなかった。
   Achikochi sagashita keredo mitsukaranakatta.
   I looked far and wide but couldn't find it.

There is another varient *atchikotchi* あっちこっち, which is a little more colloquial than *achikochi.*

AITE 相手　partner, opponent

Aite 相手 means someone with whom one does something. Depending on the activity, therefore, *aite* could be either one's partner or competitor.

1. 結婚の相手
   kekkon no aite
   marriage partner
2. 明日の試合の相手
   ashita no shiai no aite
   the opponent of tomorrow's game/match

ASAGOHAN 朝ご飯 breakfast

In English, breakfast is always breakfast, and there is no other word that can take its place. In Japanese, however, there are at least four words meaning the same thing: *asagohan* 朝ご飯, *asahan* 朝飯, *asameshi* (also written 朝飯), and *chooshoku* 朝食. *Asagohan* probably is the most common term, *asahan* is slightly less common, *asameshi* is used only by men in informal situations, and *chooshoku* is the most formal of all. All these words come as part of sets representing the three main meals of the day, as follows:

Breakfast	Lunch	Dinner
asagohan	(o)hirugohan	bangohan/yuugohan
asahan	hiruhan	yuuhan
asameshi	hirumeshi	banmeshi/yuumeshi
chooshoku	chuushoku	yuushoku

These sets require different verbs meaning "to eat." To mean "eat breakfast," for example, one can say *asagohan/asahan o taberu, asameshi o kuu,* or *chooshoku o toru,* switching from one verb to another, depending on which noun for "breakfast" is used.

⌈ATAMA⌐ 頭 head

Once a student of mine wrote *Ii atama ga arimasu* to mean "someone has a good head." In normal Japanese, however, one would say *daredare* ("so and so") *wa atama ga ii desu* instead. In fact, this pattern "A *wa* B *ga* + adj." is commonly used to describe a person or a thing, the most famous sentence being *Zoo wa hana ga nagai* "An elephant has a long trunk (lit., As for an elephant, the trunk is long.)." Other examples would be:

1. あの子は目が大きい。
   Ano ko wa me ga ookii.
   That child has big eyes.
2. 東京は人が多い。
   Tookyoo wa hito ga ooi.
   Tokyo is heavily populated.

⌐ATO あと after

The following sentence represents an oft-committed error.

1. 勉強するあとでテレビを見ます。
   *Benkyoo-suru ato de terebi o mimasu.
   After studying I watch TV.

If one wants to use a verb before *ato,* one must use the *-ta* form, whether the event reported is a past event or non-past event, as in 2 below:

2. 勉強したあとでテレビを見ます。
   Benkyoo-shita ato de terebi o mimasu.

Also, the verb must directly precede *ato.* Since *ato* functions as a pseudo-noun, there is no need to use *no,* as in 3.

3. *Benkyoo-suru no ato de terebi o mimasu.*

AU 会う **to meet, to see, to come across**

Au is never used to refer to a class period, as in 1.
1. *Nihongo no kurasu wa shuu ni go-kai aimasu.*
    The Japanese class meets five times a week.
    To convey that meaning, one has to say the following:
2. 日本語のクラスは週に五回あります／です。
    Nihongo no kurasu wa shuu ni go-kai arimasu/desu.
    Sentence 3 below, which is often directed to me by my
    American students, sounds strange (apart from the non-use
    of *keigo*) and should be restated as Sentence 4:
3. *Kyoo sensei ni ai ni kenkyuushitsu e ittemo ii desu ka.*
    May I come to your office to see you today?
4. 今日は先生にご相談したいことがあるので、研究室へ
    伺ってもよろしいでしょうか
    **Kyoo wa sensei ni gosoodan-shitai koto ga aru node, ken-
    kyuushitsu e ukagatte mo yoroshii deshoo ka.**
    Lit., Today I have something I'd like to consult you
    about. May I come to your office?
    In other words, when one goes to see one's teacher to ask
him a favor or a question, or when one goes to see one's doctor, *ai ni iku* should be avoided.

BENKYOO-SURU 勉強する **to study**

Do not use the object marker *o* twice, as in Sentence 1, to
mean "I am studying Japanese."
1. ＊日本語を勉強をしています。
    ＊Nihongo o benkyoo o shite imasu.
    Instead, use either 2a or 2b.

2.(a) 日本語を 勉強し ています。
   Nihongo o benkyoo-shite imasu.
(b) 日本語の 勉強をし ています。
   Nihongo no benkyoo o shite imasu.

This rule of not repeating *o* is also applicable to other compound verbs such as *renshuu-suru* "to practice," *ryokoo-suru* "to travel," and *shuuri-suru* "to repair."

BIKKURI-SURU びっくりする to be surprised

Bikkuri-suru, like *odoroku*, means "to be surprised," the only difference being that *bikkuri-suru* is probably more subjective and colloquial than *odoroku*.

In English, a number of verbs relating to one's emotions are used in the passive, as in "I was surprised/amazed/astonished/touched/moved/pleased/overjoyed." The Japanese counter-parts, however, all occur in the active, as in

1.(a) びっくりした／驚いた。
   Bikkuri-shita/Odoroita.
   I was surprised/amazed/astonished.
(b) 感動した。
   Kandoo-shita.
   I was touched/moved.

Although these Japanese verbs may be used in the causative-passive, as in "*Bikkuri-saserareta/Odorokasareta/Kandoo-saserareta*, etc.," they are wordier that way, sound more translation-like, and occur much less frequently.

BINBOO 貧乏 poor, needy

Whereas English *poor* has several meanings, *binboo* has only one. It is the opposite of *kanemochi* "wealthy" and is a *na-*adjective.

1. 国の経済が悪化すると、貧乏な人が増える。

   Kuni no keizai ga akka-suru to, binboo na hito ga fueru.

   When the national economy deteriorates, the number of poor people increases.

   Unlike "poor," *binboo* cannot be used figuratively to describe things such as talent, ability, and knowledge. For that, one must use another word, e.g., *mazushii* "poor" or *toboshii* "lacking."

2. 貧しい(or 乏しい)才能

   mazushii (or toboshii) sainoo

   poor talent

   Whereas "poor" is often used to express compassion, *binboo* must be replaced by another word such as *kawaisoo*.

3. 田中さん自動車事故で怪我したんだって、かわいそうに。

   Tanaka-san jidooshajiko de kega-shita n datte, kawaisoo ni.

   Mr. Tanaka got hurt in a car accident, poor man.

   Unlike *kanemochi*, which can mean both "wealthy" and "wealthy person," *binboo* can mean only "poor" and not "poor person." For the latter, one must say *binboonin*.

4. 貧乏人(*貧乏)は金持ちより心が清いかもしれない。

   Binboonin (*binboo) wa kanemochi yori kokoro ga kiyoi ka mo shirenai.

   The poor might be more pure-hearted than the rich.

BYOOKI 病気 **sick, ill**

In English, it is perfectly all right to say "I am very sick," using "very" as an intensifier. Since "very" is *totemo, taihen, hijooni,* etc., in Japanese, American students of Japanese have a tendency to say:

1. ＊きのうはとても（大変、非常に）病気でした。
   ＊Kinoo wa totemo (taihen, hijooni) byooki deshita.
   I was very sick yesterday.

This is wrong, however, because, unlike English sick, *byooki* is not an adjective, but a noun. It therefore cannot be modified by an adverb such as *totemo, taihen,* and *hijooni.* Compare this with *genki,* a *na*-adjective, which may be modified by adverbs.

2. メリーはこのごろとても（大変、非常に）元気だ。
   Merii wa konogoro totemo (taihen, hijooni) genki da.
   To intensify *byooki,* adjectives must be used instead.

3. きのうはひどい病気で一日中寝ていた。
   Kinoo wa hidoi byooki de ichinichijuu nete ita.
   Yesterday I was in bed all day because of a terrible illness.

In other words, *byooki* functions like nouns for specific illnesses such as *kaze* "a cold" and *zutsuu* "a headache."

4. きのうはひどいかぜ／頭痛で一日中寝ていた。
   Kinoo wa hidoi kaze/zutsuu de ichinichijuu nete ita.
   Yesterday I was in bed all day because of a terrible cold/headache.

CHICHI 父 father

When referring to parents, one must put *chichi* before *haha* 母 unlike in English, where "mother and father" or "Mom and Dad" is quite acceptable. In Japanese, however, whether one says *otoosan to okaasan* or *chichi to haha* to mean "Dad and Mom" or "father and mother," the word order is set and should not be changed, just as one would never say in English "pepper and salt" instead of "salt and pepper."

CHIGAU 違う **to be different**

In English, "different" is used with "from," as in "Japanese is quite different from Chinese." In Japanese, however, the particle used is *to*, not *kara*.

1. 日本語は中国語と(＊から)ずいぶん違う。
   Nihongo wa Chuugokugo to zuibun chigau.
   Japanese is quite different from Chinese.

   In English, one usually says "A is quite/much/a lot different from B," rather than "A is very different from B." Interestingly, the Japanese counterparts of "very" such as *totemo/taihen* don't go well with *chigau,* either. Other adverbs such as *zuibun* and *kanari* are preferred instead, as in

2. 大阪は東京とずいぶん／かなり違う。
   Oosaka wa Tookyoo to zuibun/kanari chigau.
   Osaka is a lot/quite different from Tokyo.

CHOKIN 貯金 **savings**

Chokin can mean either "saving money" or "saved money."

1.(a) 太郎はお年玉を全部貯金した。
   Taroo wa otoshidama o zenbu chokin-shita.
   Taro put all his New Year's cash gifts into his savings.

   (b) 太郎はあまり貯金を引き出さない。
   Taroo wa amari chokin o hikidasanai.
   Taro does not withdraw money from his savings very often.

   In Japan, savings one can keep at the post office are called *chokin* whereas bank savings are referred to as *yokin.* For some reason, therefore, nobody says **yuubin-yokin* or **ginkoo-chokin.* Actually, *chokin* is a much more common word while *yokin* sounds more professional. If you put a coin in a piggy bank, therefore, call it *chokin,* not *yokin!*

-CHUU 中 during

1. きょうは午前中とても忙しかった。
   Kyoo wa gozen-chuu totemo isogashikatta.
   Today I was very busy in the morning.
   If you use *ni* after *chuu,* the combination means "by the end of," as in:
2. 今週中にこれをやって下さい。
   Konshuu-chuu ni kore o yatte kudasai.
   Please do this by the end of this week.
   There is another suffix *-juu,* which is often written 中 also, but is used a little differently. (See -JUU.)

CHUUI 注意 attention, caution, advice

Chuui-suru often means "to pay attention" or "to be careful," as in 1 and 2.
1. 雪の日は転ばないように注意して下さい。
   Yuki no hi wa korobanai yoo ni chuui-shite kudasai.
   On a snowy day, please be careful not to slip and fall.
2. 夏は健康に注意すべきだ。
   Natsu wa kenkoo ni chuui-su beki da.
   In the summer one should pay attention to one's health.
   Sentence 3 below, however, is wrong, and has to be rephrased as in Sentence 4.
3. ＊眠いと先生の講義に注意できない。
   *Nemui to sensei no koogi ni chuui dekinai.
   When sleepy, one cannot pay attention to the professor's lecture.
4. 眠いと先生の講義に注意が集中できない。
   Nemui to sensei no koogi ni chuui ga shuuchuu dekinai.
   When sleepy, one cannot concentrate on the professor's lecture.

Chuui-suru also means "to caution," "to warn," or "to advise," as in

5. 試験であまり悪い点を取ったので、先生に注意された。

   Shiken de amari warui ten o totta no de, sensei ni chuui-sareta.

   Since I received a bad grade on the exam, I was cautioned by the teacher.

Because of this, *chuui-jinbutsu* 注意人物 (lit., caution person) means "someone we must treat with suspicion," i.e., a black-listed person.

DARE だれ who?

In English, "who" may refer to other things than just persons, e.g.:

1. In World War II, whom did Japan fight against?
2. Who beat the Yankees yesterday?

In Japanese, *dare* may not be used in the above circumstances. One would use *doko* (lit., what place) instead, as in

3. 第二次大戦のとき、日本はどこと戦ったんですか。

   Dainijitaisen no toki, Nihon wa doko to tatakatta n desu ka.

   lit., At the time of World War II, what places (i.e., what countries) did Japan fight against?

4. きのうは、どこがヤンキーズに勝ったんですか。

   Kinoo wa doko ga Yankiizu ni katta n desu ka.

   lit., Yesterday, what place (i.e., what team) beat the Yankees?

DEMO でも but

Demo meaning "but" is used at the beginning of a sentence, as in

1. 試験は難しかったです。でもがんばったから、いい点を
   もらいました。
   **Shiken wa muzukashikatta desu. Demo ganbatta kara, ii
   ten o moraimashita.**
   The exam was difficult, but I tried hard and got a good
   grade.

   Do not, however, connect the two sentences above, as in
   2 below. That would create an ungrammatical sentence.

2. *試験は難しかったでも、がんばったから、いい点をもら
   いました。
   ***Shiken wa muzukashikatta demo, ganbatta kara, ii ten o
   moraimashita.**

   To make this grammatical, one would have to use either
   ga or *keredo* as in 3.

3. (a) 試験は難しかったですが、がんばったから、いい点
   をもらいました。
   **Shiken wa muzukashikatta desu ga, ganbatta kara, ii
   ten o moraimashita.**

   (b) 試験は難しかった（です）けれど、がんばったから、
   いい点をもらいました。
   **Shiken wa muzukashikatta (desu) keredo, ganbatta
   kara, ii ten o moraimashita.**

   Please note that in 3(a) *desu* is obligatory, whereas in 3(b)
   desu is optional.

   Demo meaning "even, even though" may not follow a
   verb or an adjective, but may follow a noun, as in 4.

4. 難しい試験でも、がんばればパスできますよ。
   Muzukashii shiken demo, ganbareba pasu dekimasu yo.
   Even though the exam might be difficult, you can pass if
   you try hard.

DENWA O KAKERU 電話をかける to phone

Morita (1985) calls the following sentence not quite correct.

1. ＊電話をかけようとしたが、かからなかった。

   ＊Denwa o kake yoo to shita ga, kakaranakatta.

   I tried to reach him by phone, but could not get through.

To convey the meaning above, Morita suggests using 2 below.

2. 電話をかけたが、お話し中だった。

   Denwa o kaketa ga, ohanashi-chuu datta.

   I tried to call him, but the line was busy.

In other words, *denwa o kakeru* may be used whether or not the call goes through, whereas "to phone" may not.

According to Morita, *denwa o kake yoo to suru* describes the stage before one picks up the receiver, puts in a coin, or inserts a telephone card. The following sentence would, therefore, be acceptable, unlike 1 above.

3. 電話をかけようとしたが、電話帳が見当らなかった。

   Denwa o kake yoo to shita ga, denwachoo ga miatara-nakatta.

   I tried to make a phone call but could not find a phone book.

DERU 出る to attend; go out

One should beware of the difference between *ni deru* and *o deru*. The former means "to attend," while the latter means "to go out of" or "to leave." For example,

1. クラスに出る

   kurasu ni deru

   to attend class

2. クラスを出る

   kurasu o deru

   to leave class

DONNA HITO どんな人 what kind of person?

Although *donna hito* and *dooiu hito* are both translated into English as "what kind of person," they are not really synonymous. For example, although 1(a) and 1(b) both mean "What kind of man did Ms. Tanaka marry?", the answers will probably be different.

1.(a) 田中さんどんな人と 結婚し たの。
   Tanaka-san donna hito to kekkon-shita no.
  (b) 田中さんどういう人と 結婚し たの。
   Tanaka-san dooiu hito to kekkon-shita no.

  Question 1a is asking about the man's looks, personality, etc.; the answer will be something like 2a and 2b.

2.(a) すごく ハンサムな 人よ 。
   Sugoku hansamu na hito yo.
   A really handsome man.
  (b) ハンサムじゃないけど、ユーモアがあって面白い人よ。
   Hansamu ja nai kedo, yuumoa ga atte omoshiroi hito yo.
   He's not handsome, but he's a fun guy with a sense of humor.

  Question 1b is asking about the man's background; the answer will most likely be like 3(a) or 3(b).

3.(a) 東大出て、 外務省に 勤めているんですって 。
   Toodai dete, Gaimushoo ni tsutomete iru n desu tte.
   I hear he's a University of Tokyo graduate and works for the Foreign Office.
  (b) 彼女の 高校時代から の友達なのよ 。
   Kanojo no kookoo-jidai kara no tomodachi na no yo.
   He's a friend of hers from her high school days.

ERAI 偉い great; celebrated; praiseworthy; admirable

In his *Zoku Nihonjin no Eigo* (1990), Mark Petersen describes *erai* as one of those common Japanese words that are extremely hard to translate into English. First, *erai* means "great."

1. 両親を本当に偉いと思っていられる子供は幸せだ。

    Ryooshin o hontoo ni erai to omotte irareru kodomo wa shiawase da.

    Children who can think their parents are truly great are fortunate.

Sometimes, *erai* means "of higher rank."

2. A: 僕たちここに座ってもいい？

    Boku-tachi koko ni suwatte mo ii?

    May we sit here?

    B: そこは偉い人たちの席だからだめ。

    Soko wa erai hito-tachi no seki da kara dame.

    No, you can't. Those seats are reserved for biggies.

Such translations as "praiseworthy" and "admirable" make it sound as though *erai* is indeed a big word reserved for special occasions, but it is not so at all. In fact, it is used all the time on ordinary occasions. For example, if a child brings home a good report card from school, his/her mother might say,

3. 偉かったね！

    Erakatta ne!

    Good for you! (lit., That was great!)

If a little child falls and skins his/her knee but tries not to cry, his/her mother will definitely say,

4. 偉い、偉い！

    Erai, erai!

    Good boy/girl!

FUDAN ふだん usual

Fudan means "usual" in the sense of "occurring at normal times or in everyday situations." Sentence 1 is, therefore, correct, but Sentence 2 is not.

1. ふだんから勉強しておくと、試験になっても困らない。
    Fudan kara benkyoo-shite oku to, shiken ni natte mo ko-maranai.
    If you keep studying (normally), you won't have trouble with exams.
2. ＊健二はふだんの青年だ。
    *Kenji wa fudan no seinen da.
    Kenji is an average young man.
    In 2 above, *fudan* should be replaced by *futsuu,* as in 3.
3. 健二はふつうの青年だ。
    Kenji wa futsuu no seinen da.

FUJIN 婦人 **woman**

Fujin, meaning "woman," sounds quite old-fashioned as compared with *josei.* Until a few decades ago, women's restrooms in public places were designated as *fujin-yoo* (lit., "for women's use"). Nowadays, however, such restrooms probably just have a red logo shaped like a woman on the doors or are designated as *josei* instead. I am certain no enlightened Japanese women of today would like to be referred to as *fujin* or even *go-fujin* with the addition of an honorific prefix.

FUKU 服 **clothes; clothing**

Fuku, unlike "clothes" or "clothing," does not include underwear. *Kinoo fuku o aratta* (lit., "I washed clothes yesterday") sounds as though you washed washable dresses or suits.

Fuku usually refers to Western-style clothes such as dresses and suits, and not to kimonos. However, if one really wants to make a clear distinction between kimonos and Western-style clothes, one should use *wafuku* 和服 or *kimono* 着物 for the former and *yoofuku* 洋服 for the latter, as in

1. このごろの若者は洋服ばかりで、和服は持っている人も少ないだろう。

   Konogoro no wakamono wa yoofuku bakari de, wafuku wa motte iru hito mo sukunai daroo.

   Young men these days wear only Western clothes, and there are probably very few who own kimonos.

FURUSATO ふるさと **birthplace; home village/town**

If you asked Japanese people what words sound the best to them, I have a feeling they might choose *furusato* as one of them. *Furusato* (lit., "old home village") is indeed a poetic-sounding, nostalgia-soaked word. It is probably not very frequently used in ordinary conversation but more commonly in literary works such as poems. The same is true with *kokyoo,* which also means "old home village." The most common expression in daily conversation is *kuni* (lit. "country").

1. お盆には、ちょっとくにの両親の所へ帰ってこようと思っています。

   Obon ni wa, chotto kuni no ryooshin no tokoro e kaette koyoo to omotte imasu.

   I'm thinking of going home to visit my parents in the country for the Bon Festival.

FUTORU 太る **to become fat; to gain weight**

"To gain weight" is *futoru,* and not *futoku naru* "to become thick."

1. 吉田さんは昔ずいぶんやせていたけれど、結婚して少し
   太った（＊太くなった）ようだ。
   Yoshida-san wa mukashi zuibun yasete ita keredo, kekkon-shite sukoshi futotta yoo da.
   Mr. Yoshida used to be very thin, but he seems to have gained some weight since he got married.

Futoku naru may refer to a person's arms and legs, as in Sentence 2, but not his/her whole body.

2. あの力士はこのごろ太って、腕も足も太くなった。
   Ano rikishi wa kono goro futotte, ude mo ashi mo futoku natta.
   Recently that sumo wrestler has gained weight; both his arms and his legs have become bigger.

Since *futoru* by itself means "to become fat" or "to gain weight," it is totally unnecessary to add *naru* to express the sense of "to become." It is therefore wrong to use 3 below to mean "I have gained weight."

3. ＊私は太ってになった。
   ***Watashi wa futotte ni natta.**

GANBARU がんばる to try one's best; to stick it out

Ganbaru is a very frequently used expression, especially in its imperative form *Ganbare* or *ganbatte.* It is often used to encourage people who are about to take an exam, play an important game, etc., as in 1 and 2.

1. A. 今日は歴史の試験があるんだ。
   Kyoo wa rekishi no shiken ga aru n da.
   Today I have a history exam.
   B. そうか。じゃがんばれよ。
   Soo ka. Ja ganbare yo.
   Do you? Good luck then.

2. A. あしたテニスの試合があるんですよ。

   Ashita tenisu no shiai ga aru n desu yo.

   Tomorrow I have a big tennis match coming up.

   B. それじゃがんばってください。

   Sore ja ganbatte kudasai.

   Good luck then.

Although *ganbare* or *ganbatte* is thus used when English speakers would say "Good luck!", this usage is limited to situations where making effort is involved. If you find out a friend is going into a hospital with a serious illness, therefore, *Ganbatte!* might sound a little out of place. In such a case, *Odaiji ni!* ("Take care of yourself!") would sound more considerate.

GENKI 元気 healthy; in good spirits

In English, "healthy" can mean either "in good health," as in "a healthy person," or "good for the health," as in "a healthy drink." *Genki,* on the other hand, means "in good health" but can never mean "good for the health." Sentence 1 is, therefore, right, but Sentence 2 is not.

1. お元気ですか。

   Ogenki desu ka.

   Are you well?

2. *すしは元気な食べ物と言われている。

   *Sushi wa genki na tabemono to iwarete iru.

   Sushi is said to be healthy food.

Instead of *genki na tabemono,* one should say *karada ni yoi tabemono* "food that is good for the body" or *kenkooteki na tabemono* "healthful food."

Genki also means "vigor, energy, good spirits" or their corresponding adjectives, i.e., "vigorous, energetic, in good spirits," as in

3. うちの息子は、東大の入学試験に落ちて元気がない。早く元気になって（or 元気を出して）くれるといいんだが。
   Uchi no musuko wa Toodai no nyuugakushiken ni ochite genki ga nai. Hayaku genki ni natte (or genki o dashite) kureru to ii n da ga.
   My son is in low spirits, having failed the entrance exam to the University of Tokyo. I hope he will cheer up soon.

GIMON 疑問 a question; doubt

Although *gimon* is often translated as "question," it can mean that only in the sense of a question one has in one's mind. When that question is uttered, it becomes a *shitsumon* 質問.

1. ちょっと疑問に思ったので、質問してみた。
   Chotto gimon ni omotta node, shitsumon-shite mita.
   I had a question in mind, so I asked him.

Because of this difference, although one can say *shitsumon-suru* "to ask a question," one cannot say **gimon-suru*.

GYAKU 逆 opposite; reverse

Gyaku and *hantai* are both translated "opposite," and are often used interchangeably. For example, in Sentence 1, either may be used.

1. 急に逆 (or 反対) の方向から彼が現われたのでびっくりした。
   Kyuu ni gyaku/hantai no hookoo kara kare ga arawareta node bikkuri-shita.
   I was surprised to see him suddenly appear from the opposite direction.

However, there is a slight difference in connotation. *Gyaku* connotes "the opposite of what's normal or correct," whereas *hantai* has no such connotation. For example,

2. 一から十まで逆に言ってみてください。

Ichi kara juu made gyaku ni itte mite kudasai.

Please try saying 1 through 10 backwards.

When one recites 1 through 10, one usually does it in normal order, i.e., *ichi, ni, san, . . .* Saying the numbers backwards, i.e., *juu, kyuu, hachi, . . .* would be contrary to the norm. In Sentence 2, therefore, *hantai ni* would sound a little strange. Even in Sentence 1 above, that difference is still there. The expression *gyaku no hookoo* connotes "direction contrary to my expectation," whereas *hantai no hookoo* simply means "opposite direction."

HABUKU 省く **to leave out**

Habuku basically means "to leave out" or "to omit," as in

1. 日本語では文の主語を省くことが多い。

Nihongo de wa bun no shugo o habuku koto ga ooi.

In Japan, the subject of a sentence is often left out.

In this sense, *habuku* is very much like *ryakusu,* which also can mean "to omit." *Ryakusu,* therefore, can be used instead of *habuku* in Sentence 1. *Ryakusu,* however, is different in the sense it also means "to abbreviate," as in

2. 「テレビ」は「テレビジョン」を略したものだ。

"Terebi" wa "terebijon" o ryakushita mono da.

Terebi is an abbreviation of *terebijon.*

Habuku has no such meaning.

HAGEMASU 励ます **to encourage**

Once an American student wrote Sentence 1 in a composition.

1. ＊アメリカの先生は学生が質問をきくことを励ます。

   ＊Amerika no sensei wa gakusei ga shitsumon o kiku koto o hagemasu.

   American teachers encourage their students to ask questions.

   Aside from the fact that *shitsumon o kiku* should be replaced by *shitsumon o suru* to mean "to ask questions," the above sentence is wrong in that *hagemasu* is not used correctly. *Hagemasu* basically means "to encourage someone who is down-hearted," as in

2. 入学試験に落ちた友達を励ました。

   Nyuugakushiken ni ochita tomodachi o hagemashita.

   I encouraged a friend who flunked an entrance exam.

   Sentence 1 should probably be rephrased as below.

3. アメリカの先生は学生からの質問を歓迎する。

   Amerika no sensei wa gakusei kara no shitsumon o kangei-suru.

   American teachers welcome questions from their students.

HAGESHII 激しい violent

Hageshii in the sense of "violent" may be used to describe weather-related things such as *kaze* "wind," *ame* "rain," *arashi* "storm," and *yuki* "snow." It may also serve an adjective for *kotoba* "words," *kanjoo* "feelings," etc., as in:

1. 激しい言葉をぶつけ合った。

   Hageshii kotoba o butsuke-atta.

   They hurled fiery words at each other.

   Hageshii, however, is inappropriate for describing such things as societies and movies. For example, Sentences 2(a) and 2(b) are both strange.

2.(a) ＊のごろ 社会が 激しく なってきた。

*Konogoro shakai ga hageshiku natte-kita.

Recently society has become violent.

(b) ＊私は 激しい 映画は 好きじゃない。

*Watashi wa hageshii eiga wa suki ja nai.

I don't like violent movies.

To make these sentences appropriate, use *booryoku* "violence" or its derivatives.

3.(a) このごろ 社会が 暴力的になってきた（ or 暴力化して きた）。

Konogoro shakai ga booryoku-teki ni natte-kita (or booryoku-ka shite-kita).

(b) 私は 暴力映画は 好きじゃない。

Watashi wa booryoku-eiga wa suki ja nai.

HAIRU 入る to enter; join

Hairu has several meanings. The most common one is "to enter," as in

1.(a) 息子が 今度大学に 入りました。

Musuko ga kondo daigaku ni hairimashita.

My son just entered college.

(b) ゆうべ どろぼう に入られた。

Yuube doroboo ni hairareta.

Last night a thief entered (i.e., broke into) my house.

Hairu can also mean "to join" (such things as clubs).

2. 太郎は 高校でテニス部に 入った。

Taroo wa kookoo de tenisubu ni haitta

Taro joined the tennis club in high school.

It should be noted that English "enter" does not necessarily correspond to *hairu*.

3. トーナメントに出る（＊ 入る）つもりです。

Toonamento ni deru (*hairu) tsumori desu.

I'm planning on entering the tournament.

HAJIME はじめ **beginning**

Hajime "beginning" and *hajimete* "for the first time" sound very much alike and are therefore often mistakenly used. Sentences 1(a) and 2(a) are wrong, while 1(b) and 2(b) are correct.

1.(a) ＊日本では、新年のはじめての三日間よく おもちを 食べる 。

＊Nihon de wa, shinnen no hajimete no mikkakan yoku omochi o taberu.

lit., In Japan, they eat a lot of mochi for three days that occur for the first time in the new year.

(b) 日本では、新年のはじめの三日間よく おもちを 食べる 。

Nihon de wa, shinnen no hajime no mikkakan yoku omochi o taberu.

In Japan, they eat a lot of mochi during the first three days of the new year.

2.(a) ＊はじめて 日本語が 下手でし た 。

＊Hajimete Nihongo ga heta deshita.

lit., For the first time, I was bad at Japanese.

(b) はじめは 日本語が 下手でし た 。

Hajime wa Nihongo ga heta deshita.

In the beginning, I was bad at Japanese.

HAJIMERU 始める **to begin something**

At the beginning of something such as a meeting or a class, one may say "Let's begin!" in English. English speakers, transferring this sentence to Japanese, often make the error of saying *Hajimarimashoo*. One must use the transitive counterpart as in Sentence 1.

1. 始めましょう。
    Hajimemashoo.
    Let's begin.

Hajimaru is intransitive and means "something begins." It cannot mean "someone begins something." For the latter, the transitive *hajimeru* is required. Although, in Sentence 1 above, the object of the verb is not stated, it is clearly implied in that one wants to begin something such as a meeting or a class, hence the use of the transitive verb.

Likewise, the following sentence is also incorrect.

2. ＊冬になると、雪が降り始まる。
    ＊Fuyu ni naru to, yuki ga furi-hajimaru
    When winter comes, it starts snowing.

In this case, although there is no noun that serves as the object, the verb *furi-* is the object. The verb *hajimaru,* which is intransitive, therefore, has to be changed to the transitive *hajimeru,* as in

3. 冬になると、雪が降り始める。
    Fuyu ni naru to, yuki ga furi-hajimeru.

HAJIMETE 初めて **for the first time; HAJIMETE** 始めて **beginning something**

There are two kinds of *hajimete.* One means "for the first time" and is written 初めて, as in

1. 初めて韓国語を聞いた時、ずいぶん日本語と違うなと思った。
    Hajimete Kankokugo o kiita toki, zuibun Nihongo to chigau na to omotta.
    When I heard Korean for the first time, I thought it was really different from Japanese.

The other *hajimete* is the *te*-form of *hajimeru* and is written 始めて, as in

2. きょうはこの仕事を始めて三日目だ。

Kyoo wa kono shigoto o hajimete mikka-me da.

Today is the third day since I started this work.

These two words are not only written differently, but are pronounced differently. 初めて has an accent on the second syllable, whereas 始めて is accentless.

HAKU 吐く **to vomit; to eject out of the mouth**

Ejecting something out of the mouth is *haku,* whatever it is that comes out, e.g.,

1.(a) つばを 吐く

tsuba o haku

to spit

(b) 寒い 日には 吐く 息が 白く 見える 。

Samui hi ni wa, haku iki ga shiroku mieru.

On cold days our breath looks white.

(c) 日本の 酔っ 払いはよく 吐く 。

Nihon no yopparai wa yoku haku.

Drunks in Japan often vomit.

Haku in the sense of "vomit" is an acceptable expression, but *modosu* might be a little more genteel. *Gero o haku* is very much like English "puke" and should be avoided in polite company.

HANASU 話す **to tell; to speak**

Hanasu, unlike *iu,* is not used for uttering just a word or a sentence, i.e., it is used with reference to a whole conversation or a whole talk, or when such is implied.

1. ゆうべは友達と長い間話して（＊言って）楽しかった。
   Yuube wa tomodachi to nagai aida hanashite (*itte) tanoshikatta.
   Last night I had a good time talking with a friend.
2. 彼は「じゃ、また」と言って（＊話して）帰っていった。
   Kare wa "Ja mata" to itte (*hanashite) kaette-itta.
   He left, saying "See you!"

   When the object is a language, *hanasu,* not *iu,* is used.
3. このごろは上手に日本語を話す（＊言う）外国人が増えてきた。
   Konogoro wa joozu ni Nihongo o hanasu (*iu) gaikokujin ga fuete-kita.
   These days, foreigners who speak Japanese well have increased in number.

   When the particle is not *o* but *de,* either *hanasu* or *iu* may be used, as in the following example. However, there is a slight difference in meaning between 4(a) and 4(b), which, I hope, is clear from the translations given.
4.(a) 英語で話してもいいですか。
   Eigo de hanashite mo ii desu ka.
   May I speak/talk in English?
  (b) 英語で言ってもいいですか。
   Eigo de itte mo ii desu ka.
   May I say it in English?

   Another difference between *hanasu* and *iu* is that, while *hanasu* does not need an object, *iu* does.
5. あそこで話している（＊言っている）のは鈴木さんだろう。
   Asoko de hanashite-iru (*itte-iru) no wa Suzuki-san daroo.
   The person talking over there must be Mr. Suzuki.

HANE 羽 feather; wing

Hane means both "feather" and "wing," but the context usually makes the meaning clear, as in

1. 羽のついた帽子をかぶっている。
   Hane no tsuita booshi o kabutte-iru.
   She is wearing a hat with a feather.
2. 羽があればすぐ飛んでいきますよ。
   Hane ga areba sugu tonde-ikimasu yo.
   If I had wings, I would fly over right away.

HANTAI-SURU 反対する to oppose

Hantai-suru means "to oppose," as in
1. 平和に反対する人がいるだろうか。
   Heiwa ni hantai-suru hito ga iru daroo ka.
   I wonder if there is anybody who opposes peace.
   Hansuru, on the other hand, means "to violate." The difference between *hantai-suru* and *hansuru* should be clear from the following example.
2.(a) その法律に反対する人が多い。
   Sono hooritsu ni hantai-suru hito ga ooi
   There are many people who oppose the law.
   (b) 法律に反する行為はよくない。
   Hooritsu ni hansuru kooi wa yokunai.
   Illegal acts (lit., acts that violate the law) are not good.

HAYARU はやる to become fashionable; to become popular

Hayaru is most normally used with reference to fads and fashions, as in
1.(a) このごろ日本ではどんなヘアスタイルがはやっていますか。
   Konogoro Nihon de wa donna heasutairu ga hayatte-imasu ka.
   What hairstyle is fashionable in Japan these days?

(b) フラフープがはやったのは、何十年も前のことだった。

Furafuupu ga hayatta no wa nanjuu-nen mo mae no koto datta.

It was decades ago that hula-hoops were the rage.

Hayaru could be used about infectious diseases, too.

2. 冬になると、いつもいやな風邪がはやる。

Fuyu ni naru to, itsumo iya na kaze ga hayaru.

Every winter nasty colds become rampant.

Hayaru also means "to become popular," as in

3. あの店ははやっているらしい。

Ano mise wa hayatte-iru rashii.

That store seems popular.

You can talk about a kind of art, such as a type of music and a particular literary genre, being *hayatte-iru,* but you cannot talk about a particular person being *hayatte-iru.* For a person being popular, *ninki ga aru* is used instead.

4.(a) ビートルズの音楽は六十年代にずいぶんはやっていた (or 人気があった)。

Biitoruzu no ongaku wa rokujuu-nendai ni zuibun hayatte-ita (or ninki ga atta).

The Beatles' music was very popular in the 60's.

(b) ロナルド・レーガンは、なかなか人気のある (* はやっている) 大統領だった。

Ronarudo Reegan wa nakanaka ninki no aru (*hayatte-iru) daitooryoo datta.

Ronald Reagan was a pretty popular President.

Although both *hayatte-ita* and *ninki ga atta* are acceptable in 4(a) above, there is a difference in connotation. *Hayatte-ita* connotes that the Beatles' music was prevalent, i.e., everywhere you went, you heard it, whereas *ninki ga atta* simply means their music was popular, i.e., it was well-liked by a large number of people.

Hayaru also connotes "fashionable, prevalent, or popular over a limited length of time." In the following sentence, therefore, *hayatte-iru* is inappropriate and should be replaced by *ninki ga aru* because the sentence is about an almost timeless situation.

5. アメリカ映画は日本で日本映画より人気がある (＊はやっている)。

   Amerika-eiga wa Nihon de Nihon-eiga yori ninki ga aru (*hayatte-iru).

   American films are more popular than Japanese ones in Japan.

If you used *hayatte-iru* in this case, it would indicate that the phenomenon is just a temporary fad, which certainly is far from the fact. (See also NINKI and SAKAN.)

HEE? へえ Really?

Hee? expresses mild suprise and disbelief in response to someone's remark, as in the following dialogue.

1. A: 田中のやつ東大に受かったんだってさ。

   Tanaka no yatsu Toodai ni ukatta n datte sa.

   Did you hear Tanaka was accepted by the University of Tokyo?

   B: へえ？田中が？

   Hee? Tanaka ga?

   Really? Tanaka was?

Hee? sounds informal and perhaps should be replaced in polite speech by *E?*, which may be used in both informal and polite speech.

2. 先生(男)： 田中東大に受かったそうだよ。

   Male teacher: Tanaka Toodai ni ukatta soo da yo.

   Did you hear Tanaka was accepted by the University of Tokyo?

   生徒(男)： えっ？　田中が？

   Male student: E? Tanaka ga?

   What? Tanaka was?

The difference between *Hee?* and *E?*, however, is that the latter expresses only surprise (probably less mildly than *Hee?*) and not disbelief.

There is another interjection *Hoo?*, which may be used in either informal or polite speech and indicates mild surprise like *Hee?*, but without the connotation of disbelief.

3. A: うちの息子がおかげさまで東大に受かりました。

   Uchi no musuko ga okagesama de Toodai ni ukari-mashita.

   My son was fortunately accepted by the University of Tokyo.

   B: ほう？それはすばらしいですね。

   Hoo? Sore wa subarashii desu ne.

   By God! How wonderful!

Hoo? is usually used by middle-aged or old people. As seen in 3 above, it often carries a sense of admiration.

Finally, *Hee?* and *Hoo?* are both pronounced with a mild rising intonation at the end, while *E?* is pronounced with a jerky rising intonation.

HIATARI GA II 日当たりがいい having good exposure to the sun

When you look up "sunny" in an English-Japanese dictionary, you find among some choices *hiatari ga ii*. However, it cannot be used as in 1 below.

1. ＊きょうは日当たりがいい天気です。

   *Kyoo wa hiatari ga ii tenki desu.

   The weather is sunny today.

Hiatari ga ii is used only in reference to a sunny place, as in

2. 冬は日当たりのいい家がありがたい。

   Fuyu wa hiatari no ii ie ga arigatai.

   In winter, it is nice to live in a house exposed to a lot of sunshine.

Just to mean "It's sunny today," say one of the following.

3.(a) きょう は 日 が よく 照っている 。

Kyoo wa hi ga yoku tette-iru.

lit., The sun is shining well today.

(b) きょう は 晴れている 。

Kyoo wa harete-iru.

It's sunny today.

HIGE ひげ beard, moustache, whiskers

Although English has different words for facial hair, depending on where it grows, Japanese has just one word ひげ. If one wishes to make distinctions, however, it is possible to say the following.

1.(a) 口ひげ

kuchihige

moustache (lit., mouth *hige*)

(b) あごひげ

agohige

beard (lit., chin *hige*)

(c) 頬ひげ

hohohige/hoohige

whiskers (lit., cheek *hige*)

We used to use three different kanji for these three types of hige: 髭 for "moustache," 鬚 for "beard," and 髯 for "whiskers," but nowadays we simply write ひげ in hiragana for all of them.

HIKKOSU 引っ越す to move from one residence to another

In American English, "move" may be used to mean "to change domiciles," Japanese *ugoku* ("to move" in the sense of "to change position") cannot be used in that way. In the following example, only (b) is correct.

1.(a) *あした 新しいマンションに 動く ことになりました。

 ***Ashita atarashii manshon ni ugoku koto ni narimashita.**

 We are moving to a new apartment tomorrow.

 (b) あした 新しいマンションに 引っ越すことになりました。

 Ashita atarashii manshon ni hikkosu koto ni narimashita.

 For some reason, *hikkosu* is not used when the moving is to a different country. For example, the following does not quite sound right:

2. *定年退職してから外国に引っ越す人もいるようだ。

 * Teinentaishoku-shite kara gaikoku ni hikkosu hito mo iru yoo da.

 It seems that there are some people who move to another country after retirement.

 In that case, it is better to say *ijuu-suru,* as in

3. 定年退職してから外国に移住する人もいるようだ。

 Teinentaishoku-shite kara gaikoku ni ijuu-suru hito mo iru yoo da.

HISSHA 筆者 the writer of a particular piece of writing

A *hissha* is the writer of a particular piece of writing such as an essay or an article, especially one that expresses his/her opinion. It could be any length and is usually non-fiction. It could even be a letter to the editor of a newspaper, magazine, etc., as in

1. 日本の新聞の投書には、必ず筆者の年齢が書いてある。

 Nihon no shinbun no toosho ni wa, kanarazu hissha no nenrei ga kaite aru.

 In Japanese newspapers, a letter to the editor always includes the writer's age.

Compare this word with *chosha,* which has to be the author of a particular, usually non-fiction, book, *sakusha,* which means "the writer of a particular piece of fiction," and sakka, which refers to a professional fiction writer. (See also CHOSHA, SAKKA and SAKUSHA in *JWTU1.*)

HONTOO WA 本当は actually

Hontoo wa is different from *hontoo ni. Hontoo ni* is used like "really," whereas *hontoo wa* is used like "actually," "the fact is," or "to tell you the truth."

1. 東京のラッシュアワーの込み方は本当にすごい。
   Tookyoo no rasshuawaa no komikata wa hontoo ni sugoi.
   The rush hour crowds in Tokyo are really something else.
2. 東京の人口は九百万なんて書いてあるけど、本当は一千万以上のはずだ。
   Tookyoo no jinkoo wa kyuuhyakuman nante kaite aru kedo, hontoo wa issenman ijoo no hazu da.
   It says here that the population of Tokyo is nine million, but actually it should be over ten million.

HOO GA II 方がいい one should do such and such

Although *hoo ga ii* is often equated with English "had better," its tone is not as strong. It should probably be translated as "should."

1. 日本語が上手になりたかったら、なるべく早く始めた方がいい。
   Nihongo ga joozu ni naritakattara, narubeku hayaku hajimeta hoo ga ii.
   If you want to become good at Japanese, you should start studying it as soon as possible.

Basically, *hoo ga ii* is used when you are comparing two alternatives, one of which you are recommending. In Sentence 1 above, the speaker is comparing the option of starting early with the other option of not starting early. Thus, 方がいい fits in well. The following sentence, however, sounds strange.

2. * 外国語を 習いたいなら、日本語を 習った 方が 一番いい。

    *Gaikogugo o naraitai nara, Nihongo o naratta hoo ga ichiban ii.

    lit., If you want to study a foreign language, the alternative of studying Japanese will be the best.

In Sentence 2, the word *ichiban* "best, most" implies that there are more than two options. In such a case, use *no ga ii* instead, as in

3. 外国語を習いたいなら、日本語を習うのが一番いい。

    Gaikokugo o naraitai nara, Nihongo o narau no ga ichiban ii.

    If you want to study a foreign language, studying Japanese will be the best.

HOTTO-SURU ほっとする **to feel relieved**

Hotto-suru is not exactly the same as *anshin-suru,* its synonym. *Hotto-suru* describes a brief mental response, as in

1. 子供の熱が引いてほっとした。

    Kodomo no netsu ga hiite hotto-shita.

    I was relieved to see my child's fever go down.

Anshin-suru, on the other hand, may be used in reference to either a brief or a long-lasting state. For example, in 2 below, only *anshin-suru* would be appropriate.

2. 今健康だと言って、安心 (＊ ほっと) ばかりしてはいられない。

   Ima kenkoo da to itte, anshin (*hotto) bakari shite wa irarenai.

   Although I am healthy now, that does not mean I can remain relaxed forever.

⌈ICHI⌉ ー one

Ichi meaning "one" can stand alone only when used in mathematics. For example,

1. 一は二の半分だ。

   Ichi wa ni no hanbun da.

   One is one half of two.

   Ichi cannot stand alone in other cases, such as

2. ＊日本という国は一しかない。

   *Nihon to iu kuni wa ichi shika nai.

   There is only one country called Japan.

   To express this idea, one must say *hitotsu* instead, as in

3. 日本という国は一つしかない。

   Nihon to iu kuni wa hitotsu shika nai.

   Even *hitotsu* is not used very often since all sorts of "counters" must be used with numerals, depending on the noun referred to. Some of these are introduced at the beginning level, e.g.

4.(a) ここにえんぴつが一本(二本、三本・・・)あります。

   Koko ni enpitsu ga ip-pon (ni-hon, san-bon, etc.) arimasu.

   There is/are one, two, three ... pencil(s) here.

   (b) 雑誌を 一さつ(二さつ、三さつ・・・) 買いました。

   Zasshi o is-satsu (ni-satsu, san-satsu, etc.) kaimashita.

   I bought one, two, three ... magazine(s).

What is often not emphasized is the fact that the accompanying particle, e.g., *ga, o,* etc., does not follow the numeral plus counter; rather it precedes them. The following sentences, therefore, sound very strange. They almost sound like the direct translations of the English equivalents.

5.(a) ＊ここにえんぴつ三本があります。

＊Koko ni enpitsu san-bon ga arimasu.

(b) ＊雑誌二さつを買いました。

＊Zasshi ni-satsu o kaimashita.

ICHININMAE 一人前 one serving/self-supporting; full-fledged

Ichininmae has two meanings. First, it means "one serving" (of food), as in

1. 若い男性はすし一人前では足りないだろう。

   Wakai dansei wa sushi ichininmae de wa tarinai daroo.

   Young men probably need more than one serving of sushi.

   Although 一人 usually reads *hitori,* in this case *ichinin* is the only possible reading, i.e., "hitorimae" is nonexistent. Servings for two, three, four, etc., are *nininmae, sanninmae, yoninmae,* etc.

   Ichininmae also means "full-fledged" or "self-supporting," as in

2. 大学を卒業しても就職しなければ、一人前になったとは言えない。

   Daigaku o sotsugyoo-shite mo shuushoku-shinakereba, ichininmae ni natta to wa ienai.

   Even if you graduate from college, you are not a full-fledged adult until you are employed.

This latter kind of *ichininmae* is a fixed expression, i.e., *ichi* and *ninmae* are inseparable. Even in reference to more than one person, the same word must be used.

3.　太郎も花子も子供のくせに、口だけは一人前だ。

Taroo mo Hanako mo kodomo no kuse ni kuchi dake wa ichininmae da.

Although Taro and Hanako are still only kids, when they talk, they sound like grown-ups.

IJOO 以上 more than

Ijoo means "more than" and usually follows a noun that includes a number, as in Sentence 1, but may sometimes be attached to a non-number, as in Sentence 2.

1.　私の小学校では、一クラスに70人以上も生徒がいた。

Watashi no shoogakkoo de wa, hito-kurasu ni nanajuu-nin ijoo mo seito ga ita.

At my elementary school, there were more than seventy students per class.

2.　それ以上のことは言えない。

Sore ijoo no koto wa ienai.

I cannot say more than that.

The following sentence seems to be used increasingly often these days, especially at the end of an oral report.

3.　以上です。

Ijoo desu.

That's all.

IKEN 意見 opinion

In English, the expression "in my opinion" is used quite commonly, but the direct translation of this in Japanese, *watashi no iken de wa,* sounds quite stilted.

1. ?私の意見では、日本人は人の言うことを気にしすぎる。

   ? Watashi no iken de wa, Nihonjin wa hito no iu koto o ki ni shisugiru.

   In my opinion, the Japanese worry too much about what others say about them.

   Try other ways of expressing the above, for example,

2.(a) 日本人は人の言うことを気にしすぎると思う。

   Nihonjin wa hito no iu koto o ki ni shisugiru to omou.

   I think the Japanese worry too much about what others say about them.

   (b) 日本人は人の言うことを気にしすぎるんじゃないだろうか。

   Nihonjin wa hito no iu koto o ki ni shisugiru n ja nai daroo ka.

   The Japanese worry too much about what others say about them, don't they?

IKIRU 生きる **to live**

The English verb "to live" means (a) "to be alive," (b) "to reside," and (c) "to make a living; to lead a life." In Japanese, however, each of these requires a different verb, i.e., *ikiru, sumu,* and *kurasu,* respectively.

1. 百まで生きられたらすごい。

   Hyaku made ikiraretara sugoi.

   It is fantastic to be able to live to be one hundred.

2. 一度フランク・ロイド・ライトの設計した家に住んでみたい。

   Ichido Furanku Roido Raito no sekkai-shita ie ni sunde mitai.

   I wish I could live in a Frank Lloyd Wright-designed house once.

3. このごろ忙しく暮らしている。
   Konogoro isogashiku kurashite-iru.
   I am living a busy life these days.

ĪNOCHI 命 life

In English, "life" means, among other things, (a) "that which resides within a living thing and keeps it alive," (b) "the state of living," and (3) "a time span from birth to death." In Japanese, (a) is *inochi,* (b) is *seikatsu,* and (c) is *isshoo.*

1. 命だけは助けてください。
   Inochi dake wa tasukete kudasai.
   Please spare my life.
2. 日本の大学生の生活は、アメリカの大学生の生活と比べるとのんびりしている。
   Nihon no daigakusei no seikatsu wa Amerika no daigakusei no seikatsu to kuraberu to nonbiri shite iru.
   The life of a college student in Japan is more relaxed than that of a college student in America.
3. 一生を東京で過ごす人は珍しくない。
   Isshoo o Tookyoo de sugosu hito wa mezurashiku nai.
   People who spend their entire lives in Tokyo are not rarities.

   (See also SEIKATSU.)

ĪPPAI いっぱい one cup; IPPAI いっぱい a lot

Ippai has different meanings, depending on the accent. When it is pronounced *ippai,* with an accent on the first syllable, it means "one cup/glass," as in

1. 下戸というのは、ビールいっぱいでも酔っ払ってしまう人のことだ。

   "Geko" to iu no wa biiru ippai de mo yopparatte shimau hito no koto da.

   "Geko" refers to someone who gets drunk with only one glass of beer.

   On the other hand, when *ippai* is accentless, it means "a lot" or "full."

2. きょうはどうぞビールをいっぱい飲んで下さい。

   Kyoo wa doozo biiru o ippai nonde kudasai.

   Please drink a lot of beer today.

3. いつかすしをおなかいっぱい食べてみたいなあ！

   Itsuka sushi o onaka ippai tabete mitai naa!

   I hope I can eat a stomach-full of sushi someday!

Ippai in the sense of "one cup/glass" may be written in kanji, i.e., 一杯, but *ippai* in the sense of "a lot" or "full," is almost always in hiragana.

IPPOO DE WA 一方では on the one hand; on the other hand

Ippoo de wa is a tricky phrase in that it changes its meaning, depending on whether it is used alone or with *tahoo de wa* "on the other hand." Observe the following examples.

1. 日本では環境主義者が増えてきている。しかし、一方では資源の無駄使いも相変わらず目立つ。

   Nihon de wa kankyooshugisha ga fuete kite-iru. Shikashi ippoo de wa shigen no mudazukai mo aikawarazu medatsu.

   In Japan, the number of environmentalists is increasing; on the other hand, however, the wasting of natural resources is as conspicuous as ever.

2. 日本では、一方では環境主義者が増えてきているが、他 方では資源の無駄使いも相変わらず目立つ。

Nihon de wa, ippoo de wa kankyooshugisha ga fuete kite- iru ga, tahoo de wa shigen no mudazukai mo aikawarazu medatsu.

In Japan, on the one hand the number of environmen- talists is increasing; on the other hand, however, the wasting of natural resources is as conspicuous as ever.

Ippoo de wa used in the sense of "on the other hand," as in Sentence 1 above, may be preceded by *sono,* i.e., one can say *sono ippoo de wa shigen no mudazukai mo. . . .* When *ippoo de wa* is used in the sense of "on the one hand," as in Sentence 2, however, it can never be preceded by *sono.* Also, whereas *ippoo de wa,* meaning "on the other hand," may be used in speech, the pair *ippoo de wa . . . tahoo de wa* is bookish and does not appear in spoken language.

IROIRO いろいろ various

Iroiro and *samazama* are often synonymous, as in

1. すしと 言っても、実はいろいろな／さまざまな 種類がある。

Sushi to itte mo, jitsu wa iroiro na/samazama na shurui ga aru.

The name sushi actually covers all kinds.

Iroiro and *samazama,* however, are not quite the same. For one thing, *iroiro* is a very common word that can be used by anyone in all kinds of situations whereas *samazama* sounds more bookish and is very unlikely to be used by chil- dren. For another, *iroiro* often connotes "a lot," as in

2. いろいろな人にきいてみたけれど、分からなかった。

Iroiro na hito ni kiite mita keredo, wakaranakatta.

I asked lots of people (lit., all kinds of people), but nobody knew.

In situations such as 2, *samazama* would be out of place.

Also, *iroiro* by itself (i.e., without *na* or *ni*) is often used adverbially, but *samazama* is not.

3.　いろいろ（＊さまざま）助けていただいてありがとうございました。

　　Iroiro (*samazama) tasukete itadaite arigatoo gozai-mashita.

　　Thank you for helping me in all kinds of ways.

ISSHO 一緒 together

To issho ni is sometimes used in place of *to* alone, *issho ni* adding the meaning of "together." Thus Sentence 1 refers to the same event with or without the word *issho ni*.

1.　友達と（一緒に）宿題をした。

　　Tomodachi to (issho ni) shukudai o shita.

　　I did homework (together) with a friend.

There are some verbs that regularly take *to,* such as *kekkon-suru* ("to marry"), *deeto-suru* ("to date"), and *tatakau* ("to fight"). With these verbs, *to* used by itself and *to issho ni* would represent different meanings. For example,

2.(a) 太郎は 花子と 結婚し た 。

　　Taroo wa Hanako to kekkon-shita.

　　Taro married Hanako.

　(b) 太郎は 花子と 一緒に 結婚し た 。

　　Taroo wa Hanako to issho ni kekkon-shita.

　　Taro got married together with Hanako (i.e., they had a joint wedding).

3.(a) 太郎は 花子と デート した 。

　　Taroo wa Hanako to deeto-shita.

　　Taro dated Hanako.

(b) 太郎は 花子と 一緒にデート した。

Taroo wa Hanako to issho ni deeto-shita.

Taro dated together with Hanako (i.e., Taro dated someone, Hanako dated someone else, and they all went out together).

4.(a) 第二次大戦で 日本はアメリカと 戦った。

Dainijitaisen de Nihon wa Amerika to tatakatta.

In World War II, Japan fought America (i.e., Japan was Amerca's enemy).

(b) 第二次大戦で 英国はアメリカと 一緒に 戦った。

Dainijitaisen de Eikoku wa Amerika to issho ni tatakatta.

In World War II, Great Britain fought together with America (i.e., Great Britain was America's ally).

To issho ni is used when the two nouns that are juxtaposed with each other are compatible. For example,

4. *泥棒はお金と一緒に逃げた。

*Doroboo wa okane to issho ni nigeta.

The thief ran away with money.

Sentence 4 is wrong because *doroboo* "thief," which is juxtaposed with *okane,* is an animate noun and is therefore incompatible with *okane,* which is inanimate. To make this sentence correct, one would have to say

5. 泥棒はお金を 持って 逃げた。

Doroboo wa okane o motte nigeta.

The following sentence, however, is correct because *okane* is juxtaposed with *hooseki* "jewels," not with *doroboo.*

6. 泥棒はお金と一緒に宝石も 持って 逃げた。

Doroboo wa okane to issho ni hooseki mo motte nigeta.

The thief ran away with money and also jewels.

American students sometimes make a sentence like the following:

IU—IU · **57**

7. ＊今学期はブラウン先生と一緒に個人研究をしています。
   *Kongakki wa Buraun-sensei to issho ni kojinkenkyuu o shite-imasu.
   This semester I'm doing independent study with Professor Brown.

In Example 7, the English sentence is of course correct, but the Japanese is not quite appropriate because *to issho ni* sounds as though the student and the professor were studying together at the same level, which is not really the case. In Japanese, it would be better to phrase it as follows:

8. 今学期はブラウン先生に個人研究の指導をしていただいています。
   Kongakki wa Buraun-sensei ni kojinkenkyuu no shidoo o shite itadaite-imasu.
   This semester I'm doing independent study under the guidance of Professor Brown.

IU 言う **to say**

As a rule, *iu* takes only animate objects although the English verb "say" is often used with inanimate subjects, as in

1.(a) My watch says ten-thirty.
  (b) Today's paper says there was a terrible earthquake in Japan yesterday.

  The Japanese counterparts of 1(a) and 1(b) would not use the verb *iu,* but rather some other phrases to express the same meanings, as in

2.(a) 私の時計では十時半です。
   Watashi no tokei de wa juuji-han desu.
   It's ten-thirty by my watch.

(b) 今日の新聞によると、きのう日本でひどい地震が
あったそうだ。

Kyoo no shinbun ni yoru to, kinoo Nihon de hidoi jishin ga atta soo da.

According to today's paper, there was a terrible earthquake in Japan yesterday

⌈IWA⌉ 岩 rock

In American English, "rock" can be used to refer to even a small stone or pebble, as in "throw a rock." *Iwa,* on the other hand, refers to only large pieces. Whoever can throw an *iwa* must be at least as strong as Samson! Ordinary people could throw only an *ishi.*

1. 石（＊岩）を投げ合うけんかは危ない。

   Ishi (*iwa) o nageau kenka wa abunai.

   Rock-throwing fights are dangerous.

⌈JIKEN⌉ 事件 happening

Once an American student wrote to me in Japanese:

1. ＊何か日本人が集まる事件があったらお知らせくだ
   さいませんか。

   *Nani ka Nihonjin ga atsumaru jiken ga attara oshirase kudasaimasen ka.

   Will you please tell me if there is an event for Japanese people?

My suspicion is he looked up the word "event" in an English-Japanese dictionary, found *jiken* as the Japanese "equivalent," and used it. *Jiken,* however, carries a negative connotation, usually referring to the kind of event welcomed by the mass media such as murder, adultery, and bribery.

Since the writer of Sentence 1 above meant events such as parties, picnics, and lectures, he should have used *gyooji* 行事 instead. As a matter of fact, nowadays, the loanword *ibento* might be even more appropriate, as in

2. 何か日本人が集まるイベントがあったらお知らせください ませんか。

   Nani ka Nihonjin ga atsumaru ibento ga attara oshirase kudasaimasen ka.

JIKOKU 時刻 point of time

Jikan 時間 can mean either "amount/length of time," as in 1(a), or "point of time," as in 1(b).

1.(a) もう 時間がない。

   Moo jikan ga nai.

   We have no more time.

   (b) もう 起きる 時間だ。

   Moo okiru jikan da.

   It's already time for me to get up.

   Jikoku, on the other hand, refers only to a "point of time."

3. 時刻をお知らせします。

   Jikoku o oshirase-shimasu.

   We'll let you know what time it is (lit., the present point of time).

   Jikoku, however, sounds formal and is rarely used in speech except in the word *jikokuhyoo* 時刻表 "time table" (for buses, trains, airplanes, etc.).

JINKOO 人口 population

Jinkoo refers to the number of people within a certain geographical area. Since one of the Chinese characters representing *jinkoo* is 人, meaning "person," this word can refer only to humans although English "population" may sometimes be used in reference to animals.

In English, one usually talks about a certain population being large or small, as in

1. The population of New York City is the largest in the United States.

In Japanese, on the other hand, one talks about *jinkoo* being *ooi/sukunai* "many/few' rather than *ookii/chiisai* "large/small," e.g.,

2. 東京の人口は多すぎる（＊大きすぎる）。
   Tookyoo no jinkoo wa oo-sugiru (*ooki-sugiru).
   The population of Tokyo is too large (lit., too many).

JITSU WA 実は to tell you the truth

The most common use of *jitsu wa* is when one has to start talking about something one feels reluctant to bring up, e.g., something one feels shy about, ashamed of, etc., as in

1. A. きょうは何の用。
      Kyoo wa nan no yoo?
      What do you want to see me about today?
   B. 実はちょっと困ったことがありまして。
      Jitsu wa chotto komatta koto ga arimashite.
      The truth is (or I hate to bother you with my problem but) there's something that's troubling me.

Jitsu wa is quite different in usage from *jitsu ni* ("truly"), which is used to emphasize the degree of some quality. For example,

2. アラスカの冬は実に（＊実は）寒い。
   Arasuka no fuyu wa jitsu ni (*jitsu wa) samui.
   Winters in Alaska are truly cold.

In this context, *jitsu wa* could be used only if it were commonly believed that winters in Alaska are not cold, which is of course untrue.

JOSEI 女性 woman

Josei used to be a written expression, but nowadays it is used more and more in conversation as well, although it still sounds somewhat formal and is unlikely to be used by children.

1. 日本の女性はまだ男性と平等に扱われていない。

   Nihon no josei wa mada dansei to byoodoo ni atsukaw-arete-inai.

   Women in Japan are not yet treated the same as men.

   Whereas *onna* 女 sometimes carries a derogatory tone, *josei* never does.

JOSHI 女子 woman

Although 女 means "female" and 子 means "child," the combination of the two kanji 女子, pronounced *joshi,* does not mean "girl," but rather "human female." It is not used in reference to one female person, but rather to girls/women in general. For example,

1. あの大学には女子寮と男子寮がある。

   Ano daigaku ni wa joshiryoo to danshiryoo ga aru.

   That university has women's dormitories and men's dormitories.

   To mean "a girl," one has to use *onna no ko* instead of *joshi.*

2. あそこにいる女の子はかわいいね。

   Asoko ni iru onna no ko wa kawaii ne.

   That girl over there is cute, isn't she?

JŪGYOO 授業　class

Jugyoo means "class" in the sense of "the teaching given in a class," not "a group of people learning together and taught by the same teacher." It may therefore be used in Sentence 1, but not in Sentence 2.

1. アレン先生の授業はためになった。
   Aren Sensei no jugyoo wa tame ni natta.
   Mr. Allen's class was instructive.
2. 小学校の時のクラス（＊授業）は大きかった。
   Shoogakkoo no toki no kurasu (*jugyoo) wa ookikatta
   My class in elementary school was large.

The loanword *kurasu* (from English "class"), on the other hand, is broader in meaning and can be used in Example 1 above as well as in 2.

JŪKU 塾 after-school school

A *juku* is an after-school school for younger students, i.e., elementary through high school students. All kinds of subjects could be taught there, but there may be some *juku* that specialize in one particular skill, such as *sorobanjuku* ("abacus *juku*") and *shodoojuku* ("caligraphy *juku*"). *Juku* connotes a school attended by students from regular schools for extra work usually to improve in subjects where they are weak or to prepare themselves for entrance exams at various levels.

A *yobikoo* ("cram school") is very much like a *juku* in that it is not a regular school. There is some difference, however. First of all, a *yobikoo* is basically for *roonin*, i.e., students who have finished high school but have flunked college entrance examinations, although students who are still in high school may also attend *yobikoo* after regular school hours to better prepare for the coming entrance exam. Second, a *yobikoo* teaches only subjects required for college entrance exams; a *yobikoo* specializing only in one subject or offering non-required subjects such as abacus and caligraphy would thus be unthinkable. Third, a *yobikoo* is usually a large-sized school whereas a *juku* could be of any size. Fourth, at a *yobikoo,* students are often there all day since they have no other school to go to whereas, at a *juku,* students usually come in in the late afternoon after attending their regular school.

JUU 中 throughout

-juu is a suffix attached to a time word or a place word to mean "throughout," as in

1.(a) 夜中寝ないで麻雀をすれば、体をこわすに決まっている。

Yoru-juu nenai de maajan o sureba, karada o kowasu ni kimatte-iru.

It's only natural that you ruin your health if you stay up all night, playing mahjong.

(b) 春には日本中でお花見が出来る。

Haru ni wa Nihon-juu de ohanami ga dekiru.

In the spring, one can go cherry-blossom viewing throughout Japan.

-chuu is also written 中 in kanji, but the meaning is "among," "during," or "in the course of," as in

2.(a) 兄弟中、大学へ行ったのは彼一人だった。

Kyoodai-chuu daigaku e itta no wa kare hitori datta.

Of the children, he was the only one who went to college.

(b) 留守中どろぼうに入られた。

Rusu-chuu doroboo ni hairareta.

I was burglarized during my absence.

(c) 夏のクラスは午前中だけだ。

Natsu no kurasu wa gozen-chuu dake da.

Summer classes are held only in the morning.

What is really confusing is that this *-chuu* is pronounced *-juu* when attached to some time words, especially *kyoo* ("today") and *ashita* ("tomorrow"). For example,

3.   この宿題は今日中にしてしまわなければならない。

Kono shukudai wa kyoo-juu ni shite shimawanakereba naranai.

I must do this homework before today is over.

KAERU 帰る to return

Since the basic meaning of *kaeru* is "to return to the place where one belongs," a foreigner saying *Nihon e kaeri-tai* sounds very strange. If a foreign student, for example, goes to Japan for a year's study, enjoys his/her stay there, and wishes to go back there, he/she should say *Nihon e mata iki-tai desu,* instead.

KAGAKU 科学 science; 化学 chemistry

Kagaku, written 科学 in kanji, means "science," usually "natural science." *Kagakusha,* written 科学者, means "scientist," most likely "scholar whose field is natural science."

There is another word *kagaku* 化学 "chemistry," which is pronounced exactly the same as *kagaku* 科学. In written Japanese, there is no problem because of the difference in kanji, i.e., 化 verses 科. To distinguish them clearly in speech, however, 化学 "chemistry" is often called *bakegaku,* using the *kun*-reading of 化, as in

1.　鈴木さんは高校でバケ学を教えています。

   Suzuki-san wa kookoo de bakegaku o oshiete imasu.

   Mr. Suzuki teaches chemistry in high school.

KAKERU かける **to sit down**

Kakeru has many meanings, but one of them is "to sit down." *Kakeru* used in this sense could be written 掛ける and is short for *koshi o kakeru* or simply *koshikakeru,* both of which literally mean "to hang one's bottom." Unlike *suwaru,* which can refer to any mode of sitting down, however, *kakeru* can only represent sitting down on such things as a chair, bench, and sofa. Please study the following examples:

1.　アメリカの大学生は、パーティーでも床に座って(＊かけて)しまうことがある。

   Amerika no daigakusei wa, paatii de mo yuka ni suwatte (*kakete) shimau koto ga aru.

   American college students sometimes sit on the floor even at a party.

2.　どうぞソファーにおかけ(orお座り)ください。

   Doozo sofaa ni okake/osuwari kudasai.

   Please sit on the sofa. (See also SUWARU.)

KAKU 書く、描く、掻く **to write, to draw, to scratch**

In Japanese, "writing," "drawing (a picture)," and "scratching" all require the same verb, *kaku,* as in

1.(a)　手紙を書くのがきらいな人が増えている。

   Tegami o kaku no ga kirai na hito ga fuete-iru.

   People who hate to write letters are on the increase.

(b) 日本語教師は、絵を 描く のが上手な 方が 便利だ。

Nihongokyooshi wa e o kaku no ga joozu na hoo ga benri da.

For Japanese language teachers, the ability to draw pictures well comes in handy.

(c) 年を 取ると 、背中を 掻く のがだんだん 難しく なる 。

Toshi o toru to, senaka o kaku no ga dandan muzuka-shiku naru.

As one grows older, it becomes more and more difficult to scratch one's back.

Note that, although *kaku* could be written in three different ways (i.e., 書く, 描く, and 掻く), it is basically the same verb in that it is pronounced the same and could be written in the same hiragana (i.e., かく). The best way to remember that *kaku* could represent these three different activities would be that writing and drawing are also kinds of scratching although the tools used might be different!

In English, the verb "write" alone can mean "to correspond in writing," as in "Please write me more often." Japanese *kaku* does not function like this; one must use *tegami o kaku*, instead. Sentence 2 below is wrong.

2.   ＊暇があれば、どうぞ書いてください。

   ＊Hima ga areba, doozo kaite kudasai.

   Please write when you have time.

   To make this sentence correct, one must say the following:

3.   お暇な時にお手紙をください。

   Ohima na toki ni otegami o kudasai.

KANARAZU 必ず **without fail**

Kanarazu is used when the probability of something happening is, or should be, one hundred percent.

1. A. 明日の朝までに必ず宿題を出してくださいよ。

   Ashita no asa made ni kanarazu shukudai o dashite-kudasai yo.

   Please hand in your homework by tomorrow morning without fail.

   B. はい、必ず出します。

   Hai, kanarazu dashimasu.

   Yes, without fail.

Kitto "certainly; I am certain" is similar to *kanarazu* in that the probability of something happening is high, but the difference is that the probability *kitto* implies is not quite as high. For something that always happens without any exception whatsoever, *kitto* therefore is not as appropriate as *kanarazu,* as in

2. 人間は誰でも必ず（＊きっと）死ぬ。

   Ningen wa dare de mo kanarazu (*kitto) shinu.

   All human beings die without exception.

Whereas *kanarazu* may be used to describe a past event, *kitto* cannot.

3. 田中さんは、パーティーがあると必ず（＊きっと）来た。

   Tanaka-san wa, paatii ga aru to kanarazu (*kitto) kita.

   Mr. Tanaka never missed a party.

Kitto, however, may be used for a present conjecture about a past event.

4. 田中さんは、パーティーに呼んであげたら、きっと来ただろう。

   Tanaka-san wa paatii ni yonde agetara kitto kita daroo.

   I'm sure Mr. Tanaka would have come if we had invited him.

Kanarazu is normally not used with a negative, but *kitto* may be so used.

5. つゆには毎日必ず（＊きっと）雨が降るとは限らない。
   Tsuyu ni wa mainichi kanarazu (*kitto) ame ga furu to wa kagiranai.
   During the Japanese rainy season, it doesn't necessarily rain every day. (See also KITTO.)

KANEMOCHI 金持ち wealthy (person)

Kanemochi is often translated into English as "rich."
1. アメリカには金持ちの政治家が多い。
   Amerika ni wa kanemochi no seijika ga ooi.
   In America, there are lots of rich politicians.
   Kanemochi, however, as can be seen from the kanji used, literally means "having money," and is basically a noun meaning "wealthy person," as in
2. ニューヨークには金持ちがたくさん住んでいる。
   Nyuuyooku ni wa kanemochi ga takusan sunde iru.
   There are lots of rich people living in New York.
   Unlike "rich," which can be used figuratively in reference to things like talent, knowledge, experience, etc., *kanemochi* cannot. For those items, use *yutaka* 豊か. For example,
3. 豊かな（＊金持ちの）才能／知識／経験
   yutaka na (*kanemochi no) sainoo/chishiki/keiken
   rich in talent/knowledge/experience

-KANERU －かねる to be in no position to

-kaneru is attached to the stem of another verb to indicate that the speaker feels hesitant, or too shy, to do something. It is most often used when the speaker wishes to negate or decline something politely.

1.(a) 申しわけありませんが、ちょっと 頂き かねます。

Mooshiwake arimasen ga, chotto itadaki-kanemasu.

I'm sorry, but I'm in no position to accept this.

(b)ちょっと 分かり かねますが。

Chotto wakari-kanemasu ga.

This is beyond my comprehension.

Since -*kaneru* is affirmative in form, though negative in meaning, it sounds much less brusque than negative expressions such as *wakarimasen* when conveying essentially the same message, i.e., "I don't understand."

The negative form -*kanenai,* on the other hand, is used when someone will not hesitate to do something daring or out of the ordinary.

2. 彼は先生に対して失礼なことを言いかねない男だ。

Kare wa sensei ni taishite shitsurei na koto o ii-kanenai otoko da.

He is the kind of man who will not hesitate to say something rude to his teacher.

KANOJO 彼女 she

Basically, *kanojo* means "she," but it is often used to mean "girlfriend," also, as in

1. 田中の彼女にはまだ紹介されていない。

Tanaka no kanojo ni wa mada shookai-sarete-inai.

I haven't been introduced to Tanaka's girlfriend yet.

Strangely, the most recent use of *kanojo* is as a second-person "pronoun" in addressing a woman of equal or lower status, as in

2. 彼女、これしてくれない？

Kanojo, kore shite kurenai?

Won't you do this for me?

Although this usage does strike us as odd at first, it ceases to sound strange when we think of the fact that even *anata* originally meant "over there." Japanese speakers certainly like to communicate indirectly!

KANSHIN-SURU 感心する **to be impressed**

Kanshin-suru conveys positive evaluation. In the following examples, therefore, (a) is correct, but (b) is not.

1.(a) 彼の家の大きさに感心した。

Kare no ie no ookisa ni kanshin-shita.

I was (favorably) impressed by the huge size of his house.

(b) ＊彼の家のきたなさに感心した。

*Kare no ie no kitanasa ni kanshin-shita.

I was (unfavorably) impressed by the filthiness of his house.

In the case of (b) above, *kanshin-shita* must be replaced by another verb, as in

2. 彼の家のきたなさにあきれた。

Kare no ie no kitanasa ni akireta.

I was disgusted by the filthiness of his house.

KANTOKU 監督 **director; manager; supervisor**

In terms of movies, *kantoku* is "director," as in *Kurosawa-kantoku* "Director Kurosawa." In terms of sports, it means "manager," as in *yakyuu-kantoku.*" In terms of construction work, it means "supervisor," as in *genba-kantoku* "construction site supervisor."

KANZEN 完全 **perfect**

English speakers often use the adjective "perfect" simply to mean "excellent," as in

1. A. Did you have a good weekend?
   B. Yes, I had a perfect weekend.

The Japanese counterpart, *kanzen (na)*, however, is not used that way. Use other adjectives such as *subarashii, totemo yoi,* etc.

2. この週末はすばらしかった（＊完全だった）。
   Kono shuumatsu wa subarashikatta (*kanzen datta).
   This weekend was just marvellous.

KARA から from

English "Where are you from?" should not be translated directly into Japanese. 1(b), 1(c), for example, would be better than 1(a).

1.(a) ？どちらからですか。
   ?Dochira kara desu ka.
   lit., Where are you from?
 (b) おくにはどちらですか。
   Okuni wa dochira desu ka.
   lit., Where is your hometown?
 (c) どちらのご出身ですか。
   Dochira no goshusshin desu ka.
   lit., Where do you originate from?

KARE 彼 he

Kare and *kareshi,* in addition to meaning "he; that person," are often used to mean "boyfriend," as in

1. あれマリの彼(or 彼氏)？
   Are Mari no kare (or kareshi)?
   Is that Mari's boyfriend?

Kareshi is sometimes used informally as a second-person "pronoun" when addressing a man of equal or lower status, as in

2.　彼氏、これやってくれない？

Kareshi, kore yatte kurenai?

Do you mind doing this for me?

(See KANOJO)

KATEI 家庭 home

Katei means "home," as in

1.　暖かい家庭に育った子供は、やさしい人間になる。

Atatakai katei ni sodatta kodomo wa yasashii ningen ni naru.

Children who grow up in warm homes become loving people.

Although in English home may refer to a physical structure, as in "We finally bought a home last year," the word *katei* can never be used that way. For that, one has to use *ie* or *uchi*. *Kazoku* 家族, meaning "family," is sometimes used almost synonymously with *katei,* as in

2.　少年の不良化は家族／家庭の責任だ。

Shoonen no furyooka wa kazoku/katei no sekinen da.

Juvenile delinquency is the fault of the family/home.

The difference between *kazoku* and *katei,* however, is whereas *kazoku* refers to "members of a family," *katei* means "home," i.e., a place inhabited by the family. *Katei* also appears in a number of compounds such as

3.(a)　家庭料理

katei-ryoori

home cooking

(b)　家庭教師

katei-kyooshi

tutor (lit., home teacher)

(c) 家庭科
kateika
home economics
In these compounds, *katei* cannot be replaced by *kazoku.*

KATSU 勝つ **to win**

Katsu behaves very much like English "win" in such phrases
as below:
1.   試合／ゲーム／選挙に勝つ
    shiai/geemu/senkyo ni katsu
    to win a match/a game/an election
    In the following phrases, however, *katsu* must be replaced
by other verbs.
2.(a) 宝くじにあたる（＊勝つ）
    Takarakuji ni ataru (*katsu)
    to win a lottery
 (b)アカデミー賞を取る（＊勝つ）
    Akademiishoo o toru (*katsu)
    to win an Oscar

KAWARI 代わり **instead of; in compensation for**

Kawari (ni) usually means "instead of."
1.   若い日本人は、お茶の代わりにコーヒーを飲むように
    なってきた。
    **Wakai Nihonjin wa, ocha no kawari ni koohii o nomu yoo
    ni natte kita.**
    Young Japanese have started drinking coffee instead of
    tea.
    It is, however, sometimes used to mean "in compensation
for" or "to make up for," as in

2.(a) この 仕事はき つい 代わり に 給料がいい。

Kono shigoto wa kitsui kawari ni kyuuryoo ga ii.

This job is demanding, but (to make up for that) it pays well.

(b) 富士山に 登る のは 大変だが、その 代わり 頂上からの 眺めがすばらしい。

Fujisan ni noboru no wa taihen da ga, sono kawari choojoo kara no nagame ga subarashii.

Although it's tough to climb Mt. Fuji, (to compensate for that) the view from the top is gorgeous.

KEGA 怪我 injury

In English, to describe someone sustaining an injury, one most likely uses the passive, as in

1. I was hurt/injured in a car accident.

In Japanese, on the other hand, the active is the norm, as in

2. 自動車事故でけがをした。

Jidooshajiko de kega o shita.

I was hurt/injured in a car accident.

One could use the passive-causative form *kega o saserareta* only when one is hurt willfully.

3. あいつとのけんかで、ひどいけがをさせられた。

Aitsu to no kenka de, hidoi kega o saserareta.

When I had a fight with him, I was seriously injured.

KEIZAITEKI 経済的 economic; economical

Keizaiteki means both "economic" and "economical," as in

1.(a) 日本は 途上国に 十分な 経済的援助を 与え ている だろ
う か 。

**Nihon wa tojookoku ni juubun na keizaiteki-enjo o ata-
ete-iru daroo ka.**

Is Japan giving enough economic aid to developing
nations?

(b) 車のエンジンをふかし つづける のは、経済的ではな
い 。

**Kuruma no enjin o fukashi-tsuzukeru no wa keizaiteki
de wa nai.**

Leaving a car engine idling for a long time is not economical.

This is exactly the reason Japanese speakers of English
have a hard time distinguishing economic from economical.

KEKKON-SURU 結婚する to marry (someone)

In English, "to marry" is a transitive verb and takes a direct
object, as in "He married a beautiful woman," whereas Japanese *kekkon-suru* is an intransitive verb and takes the particle *to* instead of *o,* as in *Kare wa bijin to kekkon-shita.* There
are other Japanese verbs that take *to* whose English counterparts are transitive verbs. Some examples follow.

1.(a) 彼は 美人の 奥さんと すぐ 離婚 してしまった 。

Kare wa bijin no okusan to sugu rikon-shite-shimatta.

He divorced his beautiful wife immediately.

(b) 第二次大戦で、 日本はアメリカと 戦った 。

Dainijitaisen de, Nihon wa Amerika to tatakatta.

In World War II, Japan fought America.

KEKKOO けっこう quite

Kekkoo means "quite" and usually modifies adjectives and verbs with positive meanings.
1.(a) けっこう おいし いね。
   Kekkoo oishii ne.
   This tastes quite good (or better than expected), doesn't it?
  (b) 彼けっこう やる ね。
   Kare kekkoo yaru ne.
   He does pretty well (or better than expected), doesn't he?
   Kekkoo is somewhat similar to zuibun and nakanaka.
2.   君のガールフレンド (a) ずいぶん (b) なかなか
      (c)けっこう きれいだね。

2(a), 2(b), 2(c) all state the woman in question is quite beautiful. 2(a), however, is the highest compliment, signaling that the speaker is highly impressed. 2(b) signals that the speaker is somewhat surprised because the addressee's girlfriend is much more beautiful than expected. There is a sense of admiration implied, albeit less than in the case of 2(a). 2(c) is a somewhat risky statement. It certainly is not as strong a compliment as the other two. In fact, it might be taken to mean that the speaker had low expectations. The implication is like "She isn't bad at all, is she?

KENBUTSU 見物 sightseeing

Kenbutsu is often confused with *kankoo* 観光, which also means "sightseeing." There are some differences between these two, however. First, *kankoo* is more likely than not used as part of compound nouns, such as *kankooryokoo* "sightseeing trip," *kankookyaku* "sightseer; tourist," and *kankoobasu* "sightseeing bus." Second, *kenbutsu* is generally used as a verb with the addition of -*suru*. See the example below.

1. 京都へ観光旅行（＊見物旅行）に行って、たくさんの神社やお寺を見物して（＊観光して）歩いた。

   Kyooto e kankooryokoo (*kenbutsuryokoo) ni itte, takusan no jinja ya otera o kenbutsu-shite (*kankoo-shite) aruita.

   I went on a sightseeing trip to Kyoto and toured around visiting a lot of shrines and temples.

Third, *kankoo* implies a trip over some distance, i.e., it is very unlikely that the word is used for a little trip to a local event, while *kenbutsu* would be acceptable for that occasion as well.

2. 今日は町でクリスマスのパレードがあるから、見物（＊観光）に行ってこよう。

   Kyoo wa machi de Kurisumasu no pareedo ga aru kara kenbutsu (*kankoo) ni itte koyoo.

   There's a Christmas parade downtown today; I think I'll go see it.

KEREDOMO けれども but

Keredomo is most often used to connect two clauses whose meanings oppose or contradict each other. In such a case, the most appropriate English equivalent would be "but."

1. 日本人はみんな学校で英語を習うけれども、本当に上手な人は少ない。

   Nihonjin wa minna gakkoo de eigo o narau keredomo, hontoo ni joozu na hito wa sukunai.

   All Japanese study English in school, but very few are really good at it.

Keredomo is often used, however, just to prepare a setting for the statement that follows.

2. 寒くなってきましたけれども、窓をしめましょうか.

Samuku natte kimashita keredomo, mado o shimemashoo ka.

It has become chilly. Shall I close the window?

As example 2 shows, *keredomo* used this way should be left unsaid in English. *Keredomo* used to identify oneself at the beginning of a telephone conversation functions basically the same.

3. 三浦ですけれども、鈴木さんいらっしゃいますか。

Miura desu keredomo, Suzuki-san irasshaimasu ka.

This is Miura. Is Mr. Suzuki there, please?

Keredomo may also appear sentence-finally. Since the Japanese speaker has a tendency to leave things unsaid but rather to imply or suggest things instead, this expression is a favorite device used for that purpose, as in

4. 先生、ちょっとお願いしたいことがあるんですけれども・・・

Sensei, chotto onegai-shitai koto ga aru n desu keredomo...

Sir, I have a favor I'd like to ask you (but may I do so?).

Keredomo has two other versions: *keredo* and *kedo*. These three forms all mean the same, but the shorter the form, the more casual and colloquial it is. In writing, therefore, *kedo* should be avoided except in informal letters.

Keredomo and *ga* are just about the same in both meaning and function. For instance, *keredomo* in the four example sentences above may all be replaced by *ga*. There are, however, some slight differences. First, *ga* is probably a little more suited to writing than *keredomo*. Second, *ga* is not used at the beginning of a new sentence, while *keredomo* may be so used, as in

5.　北海道の冬はとても寒いです。けれども（＊が）夏は快適
です。

**Hokkaidoo no fuyu wa totemo samui desu. Keredomo
(*ga) natsu wa kaiteki desu.**

Winters in Hokkaido are frigid. Summers, however, are
pleasant.

Third, when two clauses are connected with *ga,* both
clauses should be in the same style, i.e., if the second clause is
in the formal *desu-masu* style, the first one should be in the
same style; if the first clause is in the plain *da* or *dearu* style, the
second clause should follow suit. With *keredomo,* this rule
need not be observed as strictly. For example,

6.　北海道の冬はとても寒いけれど（？が）、夏は快適です。

**Hokkaidoo no fuyu wa totemo samui keredo (?ga) natsu
wa kaiteki desu.**

Winters in Hokkaido are frigid, but summers are pleasant.

KIKAI 機会 opportunity; chance

Kikai basically means "a suitable time to do something."
Since the loanword *chansu* チャンス means about the same,
they are often used interchangeably, as in

1.　授業中は先生に質問する機会／チャンスがない。

**Jugyoo-chuu wa sensei ni shitsumon-suru kikai/chansu ga
nai.**

In class, I don't have a chance to ask the teacher a question.

There are a few differences between the two words. First,
unlike *chansu, kikai* is sometimes used almost interchangeably with *toki,* as in

2.　大阪へ行った機会（＊チャンス）に大阪城を見てきた。
Oosaka e itta kikai (*chansu) ni Oosakajoo o mite-kita.
When I went to Osaka, I visited (lit., took the opportunity to visit) Osaka Castle.

Second, *chansu* is often used specifically in such sports as baseball to mean "chance to score," as in

3. (sportscaster broadcasting): 七回裏チャンスがやってきました。
Nanakai-ura chansu ga yatte-kimashita.
Here in the bottom of the seventh inning, the team has a chance to score.

Third, since loanword equivalents appeal more to younger people than to older people, the former are more likely than the latter to use *chansu* when either will do.

KISETSU 季節 season

If you ask native English speakers to name the four seasons, some may start with "winter" while others may begin with "spring," i.e., there is no absolutely set order. In Japanese, however, the order is always set: invariably, it is *haru-natsu-aki-fuyu* ("spring, summer, fall, winter"). Even when the *on* readings are used, there is no difference: it still is *shun-ka-shuu-too.* The fact that the school year in Japan begins in the spring may have something to do with this, i.e., as far as the Japanese are concerned, everything starts in the spring, when cherry blossoms bloom.

KITAI-SURU 期待する to expect

Once a student of mine said about a classmate who was ill:

1. * 彼はきのう病気だったから、きょうは休むことを期待
   します。
   ***Kare wa kinoo byooki datta kara, kyoo wa yasumu koto
   o kitai-shimasu.**
   He meant "He was ill yesterday, so I expect him to be
   absent today," which would be perfectly all right in English.
   He did not realize, however, that *kitai-suru,* unlike expect, is
   used only with reference to desirable occurrences, such as
2. 田中さんからの援助を期待している。
   Tanaka-san kara no enjo o kitai-shite iru.
   I am expecting help from Mr. Tanaka.
   Sentence 1 above should be restated as follows:
3. 彼はきのう病気だったから、きょうは休むだろうと思い
   ます。
   **Kare wa kinoo byooki datta kara, kyoo wa yasumu daroo
   to omoimasu.**
   He was ill yesterday, so I think he'll be absent today.

KITTO きっと **I am sure (such and such) is the case.**

Kitto usually means the speaker is quite sure something is
the case, or something will definitely happen, as in
1. 田中さんはきっと来るよ。
   Tanaka-san wa kitto kuru yo.
   I'm sure Mr. Tanaka will come.
   Kanarazu, too, is used similarly, but it is more like
   "without fail," i.e., something happens without any exception, as in
2. 田中さんは夏になると必ず軽井沢へ行く。
   **Tanaka-san wa natsu ni naru to kanarazu Karuizawa e
   iku.**
   Every summer Mr. Tanaka never fails to go to Karuizawa.

Although *kitto* and *kanarazu* are quite similar, they are not exactly the same. *Kitto* has to do with one's conjecture, whereas *kanarazu* is used to express more objective certainties. For conjectures, therefore, use kitto, as in

3.　太郎はきのうクラスを休んだから、きっと（＊必ず）病気だったのだろう。

Taroo wa kinoo kurasu o yasunda kara, kitto (*kanarazu) byooki datta no daroo.

Taro was absent from school yesterday; he must have been sick.

For something for which no exception can be granted, use *kanarazu* rather than *kitto,* as in

4.　この学校では毎日必ず（＊きっと）制服で登校することが要求される。

Kono gakkoo de wa mainichi kanarazu (*kitto) seifuku de tookoo-suru koto ga yookyuu-sareru.

At this school, it is required that every day the students come to school in uniforms without fail.

Kitto may be used with negatives, whereas *kanarazu* is unlikely to be so used.

5.　田中さんはきっと（＊必ず）来ないよ。

Tanaka-san wa kitto (*kanarazu) konai yo.

I am sure Mr. Tanaka won't come.

（See also KANARAZU.）

KIWAMETE きわめて **extremely**

Kiwamete means "extremely" and is used as in,

1.　田中はきわめて優秀な学生である。

Tanaka wa kiwamete yuushuu na gakusei de aru.

Tanaka is an extremely fine student.

Kiwamete is a written expression and is rarely used in ordinary speech. In conversation, one would say something like 2.

2. 田中はすごく出来る学生だ。

   Tanaka wa sugoku dekiru gakusei da.

   Tanaka is an excellent student.

KOIBITO 恋人 sweetheart

Someone of the opposite sex whom one loves is a *koibito*. The term is reserved for a premarital sweetheart only, however.

1. 恋人と結婚できるというのは幸せだ。

   Koibito to kekkon dekiru to iu no wa shiawase da.

   It is fortunate to be able to marry someone one loves.

   Nowadays, other more up-to-date expressions such as *booifurendo* ボーイフレンド "boyfriend" and *gaarufurendo* ガールフレンド "girlfriend" are much more commonly used, especially in speech. The difference is that *koibito* could also be someone one secretly longs for, whereas *booifurendo/ gaarufurendo* must be friends in real life.

   Aijin 愛人 also means someone of the opposite sex whom one loves, but its implications are negative, i.e., "someone with whom one has a physical relationship other than one's spouse."

2. 自分の妻のほかに愛人を作ってしまうのは、明治のころの政治家にはかなりふつうのことだったのではないだろうか。

   Jibun no tsuma no hoka ni aijin o tsukutte shimau no wa, Meiji no koro no seijika ni wa kanari futsuu no koto datta no de wa nai daroo ka.

   Wasn't it fairly common for a Meiji politician to have a mistress-like woman in addition to a wife?

KOKYOO 故郷 hometown, birthplace

Kokyoo "birthplace" is mainly used in writing, as in
1. 東京はあまり大きすぎて故郷という感じがしない。
   Tookyoo wa amari ookisugite kokyoo to iu kanji ga shinai.
   Tokyo is so large that it does not have the aura of a hometown.
   (See also FURUSATO.)

KOMU 込む／混む to become crowded/congested

Komu is a punctual verb, i.e., a verb indicating a momentary action, in this case "to become crowded," as in
1. 休日は道路が込む。
   Kyuujitsu wa dooro ga komu.
   Roads become congested on holidays.

To indicate "something is crowded," *konde-iru* is normally used.
2. この電車込んでますね。
   Kono densha konde-masu ne.
   This train is crowded, isn't it?

In a pre-noun position, *konde-iru* is often replaced by *konda*.
4. 込んだ電車に乗ると疲れる。
   Konda densha ni noru to tsukareru.
   It is tiring to ride a crowded train.

In English, it is perfectly all right to say "Japan is a crowded country" or "Tokyo is a crowded city." In Japanese, however, the direct translations of these English sentences sound odd.
3.(a) ？ 日本は込んだ／込んでいる国だ。
   ?Nihon wa konda/konde iru kuni da.
   Japan is a crowded country.

(b) ？東京は込んだ／込んでいる町だ。

?Tookyoo wa konda/konde iru machi da.

Tokyo is a crowded city.

Apparently such places as Japan and Tokyo are too large to be described as *konda/konde iru*. If one narrows one's focus, these sentences become acceptable.

4. 日本／東京はどこへ行っても込んでいる。

Nihon/Tookyoo wa doko e itte mo konde iru.

No matter where one goes within Japan/Tokyo, it's crowded.

KOOFUKU 幸福 happy/happiness

Koofuku is a noun meaning "happiness" but is also used as a *na*-adjective. *Koofuku* usually refers to a person's happy state over a long period of time. For example, Sentence 1 below is correct but 2 sounds a little odd because the sentence is about happiness for a short period of time. In this sense, *koofuku* is different from English "happy," which may be used in either way.

1. ジョージは幸福な一生を送った。

Jooji wa koofuku na isshoo o okutta.

George lived a happy life.

2. ？ジョージはきのう幸福な一日を送った。

?Jooji wa kinoo koofuku na ichinichi o okutta.

George had a happy day yesterday.

Tanoshii 楽しい, too, is often equated with "happy," as in 3 below.

3. ジョージは楽しい一生を送った。

Jooji wa tanoshii isshoo o okutta.

George lived a happy life.

There is a difference in connotation between 1 and 3. *Koofuku* refers to a mentally or spiritually satisfied state, whereas *tanoshii* connotes "having fun" or "enjoying one-self." In Sentence 1, therefore, George was likely to be blessed with a nice family, trustworthy friends, a good job, etc., which gave him inner contentment; Sentence 3, on the other hand, focuses on George having had a great time all through his life—enjoying his hobbies, for example.

Sentence 2 above becomes totally legitimate if *koofuku na* is replaced by *tanoshii.*

4. ジョージはきのう楽しい一日を送った。

Jooji wa kinoo tanoshii ichinichi o okutta.

George had a happy (i.e., fun-filled) day yesterday. (See also TANOSHII in *JWTU1.*)

KOOYOO 紅葉 **fall colors (lit., red leaves)**

Kooyoo means "fall colors." Since the two characters 紅葉 stand for "red," and "leaves," respectively, they literally mean "red leaves" and, strictly speaking, should not refer to "yellow leaves," which are written 黄葉 and also pronounced *kooyoo.* 紅葉, however, is normally used broadly to include yellow leaves as well, as in

1. 日光へ紅葉を見に行きましょうか。

Nikkoo e kooyoo o mi ni ikimashoo ka.

Shall we go to Nikoo to see the fall colors?

Momiji, written either in hiragana もみじ or with the same combination as *kooyoo* 紅葉 also may refer to fall colors. *Momiji,* however, has another meaning, i.e., "maple."

2. 家の庭にもみじの木を植えた。

Uchi no niwa ni momiji no ki o ueta.

We planted a maple tree in our yard.

In this particular use, *momiji* is synonymous with *kaede* 楓 "maple." *Kooyoo* 紅葉, on the other hand, can never mean "maple."

There is an interesting word *momijigari* 紅葉狩り "excursion for viewing fall colors" (lit. "hunting for fall colors").

3. 日光へ紅葉狩りに行きましょうか。

Nikkoo e momijigari ni ikimashoo ka.

Shall we go to Nikko to view the fall colors?

Kooyoo can never be used with *-gari;* i.e., the word **kooyoogari* simply does not exist.

KOSHI 腰 **waist; lower back**

When a gym teacher calls out the following, *koshi* means "waist":

1. 手を腰に！

Te o koshi ni!

Put your hands on your waist!

In terms of size or style, especially with reference to Western-style clothing, however, *uesuto* ウエスト, a loanword from English "waist," is used instead of *koshi.* For example,

2.(a) ウエスト（＊腰）は何センチですか。

Uesto (*koshi) wa nan-senchi desu ka.

How many centimeters is your waist?

(b) あのモデルのウエスト（？腰）ずいぶん細いね。

Ano moderu no uesto (?koshi) zuibun hosoi ne.

That fashion model's waist is extremely slim, isn't it?

If someone makes the following complaint, however, *koshi* refers to the lower back.

3. 腰は痛いんです。

Koshi ga itai n desu.

My lower back hurts.

Before World War II, there were a large number of *koshi no magatta roojin,* "old people with a bent lower back," in Japan, but thanks to an improved lifestyle including better nutrition, old Japanese people nowadays seem to have better posture.

An interesting koshi-related idiom is *koshi ga hikui* "humble, modest" (lit., someone's back is low). A humble/modest Japanese frequently bows (sometimes even excessively), an act that keeps his/her lower back rather low. Hence the expression. Needless to say, the opposite is *koshi ga takai,* meaning "haughty."

KOTO GA ARU ことがある "to have had the experience of doing (such and such)"

Koto ga aru, when preceded by a V-*ta* form, is often translated as "have done (such and such)," as in

1.　私は富士山に一度登ったことがある。
   Watashi wa Fujisan ni ichido nobotta koto ga aru.
   I have climbed Mt. Fuji once.

This does not always mean, however, that English "have done (such and such)" may always be translated as -*ta koto ga aru.* For example,

2.　A: Have you done your homework yet?
   B: Yes, I've already done it.

In 2 above, "have done" is correct in English because "have done" can express not only past experience but completion as well. When you translate 2 into Japanese, however, don't use -*ta koto ga aru,* which can express only past experience, not completion. See 3 below.

3.　A: もう宿題やりましたか (＊やったことがありますか)
   Moo shukudai yarimashita ka (*yatta koto ga arimasu ka).
   Have you done your homework yet?
   B: ええ、もうやりました (＊やったことがあります)。
   Ee, moo yarimashita (*yatta koto ga arimasu).
   Yes, I've already done it.

A question using -*ta koto ga arimasu ka* is best translated as "Have you ever done (such and such)?"

4. A: 富士山に登ったことがありますか。
    Fujisan ni nobotta koto ga arimasu ka.
    Have you ever climbed Mt. Fuji?
    B: ええ、ありますよ。去年登ったんです。
    Ee, arimasu yo. Kyonen nobotta n desu.
    Yes, I have. I climbed it last year.

KUBI 首 neck, head

Kubi usually means "neck," as in

1. 首が長い/狭い/太い/細い
    Kubi ga nagai/mijikai/futoi/hosoi.
    (Someone) has a long/short/thick/slender neck.

Sometimes, however, *kubi* is interchangeable with *atama* "head," as in

2. 首 (or 頭) を振る。
    Kubi (or **Atama**) **o furu.**
    (Someone) shakes his/her head.

Although in 2 above, either *kubi* or *atama* may be used, *kubi* is probably more common. The difference between English and Japanese here is that, in English, "shake one's head" always means "move one's head sideways," and never "move one's head vertically," whereas, in Japanese, *kubi/atama o furu,* especially if accompanied by *tate ni,* "vertically," could mean "nod one's head," as in

3. 首 (or 頭) を縦に振る。
    Kubi (or **Atama**) **o tate ni furu.**
    (Someone) nods his/her head.

If one therefore wishes to make it absolutely clear that sideways motion is meant, one should include *yoko ni* 横に "sideways," as in

4.   首 (or 頭) を横に振る。

Kubi (or Atama) o yoko ni furu.

(Someone) shakes his/her head.

Although *kubi* and *atama* are interchangeable in 2 through 4 above, they are usually totally separate in use. For example, in 5(a) and 5(b) below, they refer to different parts of the body.

5.(a) 頭が痛い。

Atama ga itai.

My head hurts.

(b) 首が痛い。

Kubi ga itai.

My neck hurts.

Kubi, even when it means "head," cannot, at least in one case, be replaced by *atama.* Sentence 6 below, an order that might have been given by a samurai general to a retainer, is an example of that.

6.   敵の大将の首 (＊頭) を取って来い！

Teki no taishoo no kubi (*atama) o totte koi!

Go get the enemy general's head!

KUU 食う **to eat**

Kuu is vulgar for *taberu* and is, as a rule, used only by men. Therefore, to mean "I've already eaten dinner," 1(a) below can be used by both men and women, while 1(b) is most likely used by men only.

1.(a) 晩ご飯はもう食べた。

Bangohan wa moo tabeta.

(b) 晩飯はもう食ったよ。

Banmeshi wa moo kutta yo.

Women as well as men regularly use *kuu* to refer to eating done by little bugs and the like or as a part of such idioms as *gasorin o kuu* "eat up gas."

2.(a) 昔はよく ...- に食われたものです。

  Mukashi wa yoku nomi ni kuwareta mono desu.

  Long ago, we used to be bitten by fleas quite often.

 (b) 大きな車はガソリンを食うからだめです。

  Ookina kuruma wa gasorin o kuu kara dame desu.

  Big cars are no good because they eat up gas.

KUYASHII くやしい ?mortifying

Kuyashii is a very common colloquial expression used all the time, even by children. Yet, when one looks up the word in a Japanese-English dictionary, one finds difficult words such as "vexing," "vexatious," and "mortifying" that are hardly ever used in English conversation. The reason is simple. It is because there is no corresponding colloquial English equivalent. Mark Petersen explains *kuyashii* as "a certain mixture of anger and frustration and bitter resentment (over a perceived injustice to oneself)."

I believe one reason for the lack of appropriate equivalents is that, in English, one would often just curse in situations where *kuyashii* would be called for in Japanese. Suppose you are insulted in front of others, for example. When an English speaker recalls the incident later, he will perhaps mumble to himself things like "Damn, he was so insulting, that s.o.b.!" whereas a Japanese speaker would say *Kuyashikatta na!* When an English speaker loses a close tennis match, he will keep repeating "Damn! Damn! Damn!" in his mind while a Japanese speaker would inwardly feel *Kuyashii!*

KYOOJU 教授 **professor; instruction**

Kyooju in the sense of "professor" is discussed in *JWTU1*. The same word may also mean "instruction" but is rarely used in this sense in conversation except at a very formal level, as in

1. 先生に茶道のご教授を賜りたいのですが。

   Sensei ni sadoo no gokyooju o tamawaritai no desu ga.

   Would you be so kind as to give me lessons in the tea ceremony?

   In more normal speech, one would say something like

2. 先生に茶道を教えて頂きたいのですが。

   Sensei ni sadoo o oshiete itadakitai no desu ga.

   Would you please teach me the tea ceremony?

   When *kyooju* is used to mean "instruction," it is normally combined with other words, as in *kojinkyooju* 個人教授 "individual instruction" and *kyoojuhoo* 教授法 "teaching method," as in

3.(a) 姉は 80 以上になる のに、まだピアノ の個人教授をして いる。

   Ane wa 80-ijoo ni naru noni, mada piano no kojinkyooju o shite iru.

   Although my sister is over 80, she still gives private piano lessons.

 (b) このごろは 日本語の教授法を 勉強する 人が増えている 。

   Konogoro wa Nihongo no kyoojuhoo o benkyoo-suru hito ga fuete iru.

   Lately an increasing number of people are studying how to teach Japanese.

   In the following sentence, therefore, use *jugyoo* 授業 "teaching classes," not *kyooju* 教授.

4. 先生はこのごろ授業(＊教授)でお忙しいでしょう。

   Sensei wa konogoro jugyoo (*kyooju) de oisogashii de-shoo.

   These days you must be busy teaching.

   (See also JUGYOO in *JWTU1*.)

KYOOMI 興味 interest

Kyoomi meaning "interest" is most typically used in the phrase *ni kyoomi ga aru* "to be interested in something," as in

1. 私は子供のころから英語に興味があった。

   Watashi wa kodomo no koro kara Eigo ni kyoomi ga atta.

   I have been interested in English since I was little.

   There is another word *kanshin* 関心, which is similar in meaning to *kyoomi*.

   According to *Ruigo Reikai Jiten,* pp.302–303, *kyoomi* is emotive while *kanshin* is more intellectual. That is probably why *kanshin* sounds better in 2 than *kyoomi*.

2. アメリカ人の日米貿易に対する関心(not　興味)は、前ほど強くないようだ。

   Amerikajin no Nichibeibooeki ni taisuru kanshin (*kyoomi) wa mae hodo tsuyoku nai yoo da.

   Americans do not seem to be as strongly interested in (or concerned about) U.S.-Japan trade as before.

   There is an expression *kyoomibukai* "of deep/great interest." In this word, *kyoomi* may not be replaced by *kanshin*.

3. 中学のころ漱石の『こころ』を興味(＊関心)深く読んだ。

   Chuugaku no koro Sooseki no "Kokoro" o kyoomi (*kanshin) bukaku yonda.

   When I was in middle school, I read Soseki's *Kokoro* with great interest.

MADA まだ still, not yet

Basically, *mada* indicates that no change has taken place, as in
1.(a) まだ寒い。
   Mada samui desu.
   It's still cold. (i.e., It was cold before, and the situation hasn't changed.)
 (b) まだあったかくならない。
   Mada attakaku naranai.
   It hasn't become warm yet. (i.e., It was not warm before, and the situation hasn't changed.)

Mada is often mistakenly used with *deshita* rather than *desu* by English speakers in situations such as the following:
2. Teacher: もう宿題しましたか。
   Moo shukudai shimashita ka.
   Have you done the homework yet?
   Student:＊いいえ、まだしませんでした。
   ＊Iie, mada shimasen deshita.
   No, I haven't done it yet.

Iie, mada shite imasen is the correct answer in this case. Since the question is in the past tense, students feel tempted to answer in the past tense, too. The *-ta* form, however, is not really a past tense form, but rather a perfective. Since the act of doing the homework has not taken place, *-ta* is not used in the answer. A much simpler form *Iie, mada desu* is used quite often, too.

MADO 窓 window

Mado means "window," as in
1. この窓から富士山が見えますか。
   Kono mado kara Fujisan ga miemasu ka.
   Can you see Mt. Fuji from this window?

A store window used specifically for a display is not *mado,* but *shoowindoo* "show window" or simply *windoo,* as in

2. クリスマスのころのデパート の(ショ ー)ウィンド ー(＊ 窓) はきれいだ。

Kurisumasu no koro no depaato no (shoo)windoo (*mado) wa kirei da.

Department store show windows at Christmas time are pretty.

Windows for customers at such places as banks, post offices, and railroad stations are called *madoguchi* rather than *mado.*

3. 切手は一番の窓口(＊ 窓)で売っています。

Kitte wa ichiban no madoguchi (*mado) de utte imasu.

Postage stamps are sold at Window #1.

Incidentally, there is a humorous euphemism using *mado,* i.e.,

4. 社会の窓があいていますよ。

Shakai no mado ga aite imasu yo.

Your fly is open. (lit., Your window to the world is open.)

The person cautioned this way may not feel as embarassed as he could be.

MAI- 毎 every

Mai- is a prefix attached to certain words indicating units of time, e.g., *mainichi* 毎日, *maiasa* 毎朝, *maiban* 毎晩, *maishuu* 毎週, *maitsuki* 毎月, and *maitoshi* 毎年.

1. 日本人は毎日三回食事をするのがふつうだ。

Nihonjin wa mainichi sankai shokuji o suru no ga futsuu da.

Japanese people normally eat three meals every day.

毎月 and 毎年 have two readings each. 毎月 can be either *maitsuki* or *maigetsu;* 毎年 may be pronounced either *maitoshi* or *mainen*.

Words attached to *mai-* are usually one-character words, as seen above. One may sometimes hear such combinations as *mainichiyoobi* 毎日曜日 "every Sunday" and *maigakunen* 毎学年 "every school year," but they are rather rare. It is more normal to use *gotoni* in such cases, e.g.,

2.　メリーは日曜日ごとに教会へ行く。

Merii wa nichiyoobi gotoni kyookai e iku.

Mary goes to church every Sunday.

Do not use *-mai* with non-time words. For example, don't say *maikoku *毎国 to mean "every country" or *mainihonjin *毎日本人 to mean "every Japanese." In such cases, use other expressions such as

3.(a)　どこの国にも国旗がある。

Doko no kuni ni mo kokki ga aru.

Every country has a national flag.

  (b)　日本人は誰でも (or みんな) 富士山が大好きだ。

Nihonjin wa dare demo (or minna) Fujisan ga daisuki da.

Every Japanese person loves Mt. Fuji.

MAMORU 守る **to keep, observe, protect**

Mamoru means "to keep," but only in the sense of "to observe," i.e., "not to break."

1.　約束は守らなければならない。

Yakusoku wa mamoranakereba naranai.

Promises must be kept.

Mamoru cannot be used in the following sentence because "keep" in the following case means "to retain," not "to observe."

2. ＊図書館の本を守ってはいけない。

   ＊Toshokan no hon o mamotte wa ikenai.

   One must not keep library books.

   Most normally, this idea would be expressed instead as in 3 below.

3. 図書館の本は返さなければいけない。

   Toshokan no hon wa kaesanakereba ikenai.

   One must return library books.

   Mamoru may be correctly used as follows:

4.(a) 法律は守るべきものだ。

   Hooritsu wa mamoru beki mono da.

   Laws are to be observed/followed.

  (b) クリスチャンはキリストの教えを守るはずだ。

   Kurisuchan wa Kirisuto no oshie o mamoru hazu da.

   Christians should observe/obey Christ's teachings.

   Mamoru also means "to protect/defend."

5. 戦争は自分の国を守るためだけとは限らない。

   Sensoo wa jibun no kuni o mamoru tame dake to wa kagi-ranai.

   Wars are not just for defending one's country.

   Mamoru used in this sense may be written 護る, as well.

MARUDE まるで just like; completely

Marude has two basic meanings: (a) "just like" and (b) "completely." When it is used in the first sense, it is often, though not always, accompanied by *yoo* or *mitai,* both meaning "like." See 1(a) and 1(b) below.

1.(a) スミスさんは日本語が上手で、まるで日本人（のよう）だ。

   Sumisu-san wa Nihongo ga joozu de, marude Nihonjin (no yoo) da.

   Mr. Smith's Japanese is so good he is just like a Japanese person.

(b) あの老人はまるで赤ん坊（みたい）だ。

Ano roojin wa marude akanboo (mitai) da.

That old man is just like a baby.

Marude in the sense of "completely" is used with negative forms, as in 2(a), or with words with negative meanings, as in 2(b).

2.(a) 今日の試験はまるで分からなかった。

Kyoo no shiken wa marude wakaranakatta.

I didn't understand today's exam at all.

(b) 今日の試験はまるでだめだった。

Kyoo no shiken wa marude dame datta.

Today's exam was totally beyond me.

Marude in this sense is synonymous with *mattaku* and *zenzen* but is not exactly the same. First, *marude* implies the speaker's negative judgment, whereas the other two do not. For example, in 3(a) all three variants would be acceptable, but in 3(b) *marude* sounds a little strange.

3.(a) フランスへ行った時、フランス語がまるで／全く／全然分からなくて困った。

Furansu e itta toki, Furansugo ga marude/mattaku/zenzen wakaranakute komatta.

When I went to France, I had a hard time because I didn't understand French at all.

(b) 下手なフランス語を話すくらいなら、全く／全然／？まるで話せない方がいいとフランス人は言う。

Heta na Furansugo o hanasu kurai nara, mattaku/zenzen/?marude hanasenai hoo ga ii to Furansujin wa iu.

The French say that not being able to speak any French at all is better than speaking bad French.

Marude is different from *mattaku* in that the former has to be used with negative forms or with words of negative orientation, while *mattaku* can be used in affirmative sentences as well. In 4 below, *mattaku* may not be replaced by *marude*.

4. 富士山の眺めは全く（＊まるで）すばらしかった。

Fujisan no nagame wa mattaku (*marude) subarashi-katta.

The view of Mt. Fuji was totally fantastic.

MASHI まし the better of two poor options

If one looks up *mashi* in a small Japanese-English dictionary, all one can find is the definition "better." That is misleading. *Mashi* is used only when there are two poor options, of which one is better than the other, e.g.,

1. あんな物を食べるくらいなら、何も食べない方がましだ。

   Anna mono o taberu kurai nara, nani mo tabenai hoo ga mashi da.

   I'd rather not eat anything than eat terrible food like that.

   To compare two good options, use *hoo ga ii,* as in

2. このレストランではすしもてんぷらもおいしいけれど、どちらかと言うとすしの方がいいと思う。

   Kono resutoran de wa sushi mo tenpura mo oishii keredo, dochira ka to iu to, sushi no hoo ga ii to omou.

   At this restaurant, both the sushi and the tempura are good, but if one had to choose, I would say the sushi is better.

   In order to use *mashi* in Sentence 2, the first half of it would have to be changed, as follows:

3. このレストランではすしもてんぷらもまずいけれど、どちらかと言うとすしの方がましだと思う。

   Kono resutoran de wa sushi mo tenpura mo mazui keredo, dochira ka to iu to sushi no hoo ga mashi da to omou.

   At this restaurant, both the sushi and the tempura are bad, but if one had to choose, I'd say the sushi is the more tolerable of the two.

MATTAKU 全く entirely, totally, truly

Mattaku is quite similar to *zenzen* when used with negative forms or with words of negative orientation, as in

1.(a) 私はロシア語が全く／全然できない。
   Watashi wa Roshiago ga mattaku/zenzen dekinai.
   I don't know any Russian at all.

  (b) 私はロシア語が全く／全然だめだ。
   Watashi wa Roshiago ga mattaku/zenzen dame da.
   I am truly hopeless at Russian.

One big difference between these two expressions, however, is that *mattaku* can be used affirmatively whereas *zenzen,* as a rule, cannot, except in fun (See ZENZEN in *JWTU1*).

2. 富士山の頂上からの眺めは全く（＊全然）すばらしかった。
   Fujisan no choojoo kara no nagame wa mattaku (*zenzen) subarashikatta.
   The view from the top of Mt. Fuji was simply fantastic.

MAWARI 周り around

English-speaking students of Japanese tend to equate *mawari* with English "around" and make sentences such as

1. 日本人の友達にキャンパスの周りを見せてあげました。
   Nihonjin no tomodachi ni kyanpasu no mawari o misete agemashita.

to mean "I showed a Japanese friend around campus." Sentence 1 is grammatically correct, but the problem is *kyanpasu no mawari* means "the surroundings of the campus," which, by definition, excludes the campus itself, whereas "around campus" is similar to "all over campus" and definitely refers to the campus itself. The Japanese equivalent of "I showed a Japanese friend around campus" is

2. 日本人の友達にキャンパスを案内してあげました。

   Nihonjin no tomodachi ni kyanpasu o annai-shite age-mashita.

Sentence 3, which was once made by a student of mine, contains the same kind of problem as Sentence 1.

3. 家事というのは、家の周りの仕事です。

   Kaji to iu no wa, ie no mawari no shigoto desu.

With this sentence, the student meant "Household chores are chores around the house." Since *ie no mawari* means "the surroundings of the house," however, *ie no mawari no shigoto* can only indicate chores such as gardening and sweeping just outside the house, and not chores such as cooking, house cleaning, and washing clothes. The student should have said, *ie no shigoto* rather than *ie no mawari no shigoto*.

Mawari can be translated as "around" in such sentences as follows:

4.(a) 地球の周りを回っている人工衛星の数は大変なものだそうだ。

   Chikyuu no mawari o mawatte-iru jinkooeisei no kazu wa taihen na mono da soo da.

   I understand that the number of man-made satellites flying around the earth is astounding.

  (b) 芭蕉は池の周りを歩きながら俳句を作ったことがある。

   Bashoo wa ike no mawari o aruki nagara haiku o tsuku-tta koto ga aru.

   Basho once composed a haiku, walking around a pond.

MAZU まず first of all

Mazu usually means "first of all," as in

1. 私は朝起きるとまず顔を洗う。

   Watashi wa asa okiru to mazu kao o arau.

   After I get up in the morning, I wash my face first of all.

When used in this sense, *mazu* is synonymous with *daiichi ni, saisho ni,* or *hajime ni. Mazu* may be used either by itself or in combination with these words, as in

2. 私は朝起きるとまず第一に／最初に／初めに顔を洗う。

   Watashi wa asa okiru to mazu daiichi ni/saisho ni/hajime ni kao o arau.

Mazu has another meaning, which is similar to *daitai* or *tabun,* as in

3. 田中は東大に入りたがっているが、まずだめだろう。

   Tanaka wa Toodai ni hairitagatte iru ga, mazu dame daroo.

   Tanaka wants to get into the University of Tokyo, but he probably won't make it.

This second meaning is an extended one from the primary meaning of "first." The implication in Sentence 3 is: "When I think about Tanaka's wish to get into the University of Tokyo, my first guess would be that he won't make it."

MAZUI まずい bad-tasting; unwise, awkward

Mazui most frequently is the opposite of *oishii* "tasty."

1. 学生食堂のカレーはまずいから、外へ食べに行こう。

   Gakuseishokudoo no karee wa mazui kara, soto e tabe ni ikoo.

   The curry in the college cafeteria tastes bad; let's go out to eat somewhere else.

Figuratively, *mazui* can describe non-food items. For example,

2. 宿題を忘れたのはまずかった。

   Shukudai o wasureta no wa mazukatta.

   It was unwise/awkward to forget my homework.

MAZUSHII 貧しい **needy, poor, meager**

Mazushii can be used in two ways. First, it works as a synonym for *binboo*.

1. 貧しい(or貧乏な)家に生まれた人はかわいそうだ。
   Mazushii (or Binboo na) ie ni umareta hito wa kawaisoo da.
   I feel sorry for those who are born into poor families.
   In this usage, *mazushii* sounds more formal than *binboo*.
   Second, *mazushii* can be used figuratively to refer to non-money matters.

2.(a) 貧しい才能
   Mazushii sainoo
   meager talent

 (b) 貧しい経験
   Mazushii keiken
   meager experience

Mazushii used in this sense cannot be replaced by *binboo*. (See also BINBOO.)

MENDOO 面倒 **troublesome, bothersome; care**

Mendoo is usually a *na*-adjective.

1. 通関のためには、いつも面倒な手続きが必要だ。
   Tsuukan no tame ni wa, itsumo mendoo na tetsuzuki ga hitsuyoo da.
   For customs clearance, a troublesome procedure must always be followed.
   Mendoo may also be used as a noun meaning "care."

2. このごろの日本の若者は親の面倒を見たがらないそうだ。
   Konogoro no Nihon no wakamono wa oya no mendoo o mitagaranai soo da.
   Young Japanese today do not want to take care of their parents, I hear.

In this second meaning, however, *mendoo* is always used with *miru* and never by itself. In 3 below, one must use *mendoo o miru* or *sewa,* but not *mendoo* by itself.

3.　和子は母親の世話で(or面倒を見ることで)疲れている。

Kazuko wa hahaoya no sewa de (or mendoo o miru koto de) tsukarete iru.

Kazuko is tired from taking care of her mother.

MIERU 見える **to be visible**

Although *mieru* is sometimes translated as "can see," as in 1 below, it is not the same as *mirareru* "can see," which is the potential form of *miru.*

1.　あ、向こうに湖が見える！

A, mukoo ni mizuumi ga mieru!

Look, I can see a lake over there!

Mieru means "something is visible regardless of one's intention," whereas *mirareru* implies one's wish/effort to see something. In Sentence 1 above, where a lake just naturally came into view, *mirareru* would sound odd. (See also MIRARERU.)

MINNA みんな **everyone, all**

Minna, like its less colloquial version *mina,* is normally not followed by *wa,* though sometimes preceded by it. 1(a) is therefore correct, but 1(b) is not.

1.(a)　家族はみんな (or みな) 元気です。

Kazoku wa minna (or mina) genki desu.

(The members of) my family are all well.

(b) ＊家族みんな (or みな) は元気です。

Minna/mina may be used in conjunction with inanimate objects, too.

2. 餅はもうみんな(or みな)食べてしまった。

   Mochi wa moo minna (or **mina**) **tabete shimatta.**

   We've already eaten all the mochi.

MIRARERU 見られる **can be seen**

Mirareru is the potential form of *miru.*

1. 東京ではいろいろな国の映画が見られる。

   Tookyoo de wa iroiro na kuni no eiga ga mirareru.

   In Tokyo, one can see films from lots of countries.

   Mirareru is also the passive form of *miru.*

2. 悪いことをしているところを人に見られるのは困る。

   Warui koto o shite iru tokoro o hito ni mirareru no wa komaru.

   It's embarrassing to been seen by others while doing something bad.

   Because of this double function of *mirareru,* a large number of young people (and sometimes not so young people, as well) have started using *mireru* instead of *mirareru* for the potential form. Instead of 1 above, they would say:

3. 東京ではいろいろな国の映画が見れる。

   Tookyoo de wa iroiro na kuni no eiga ga mireru.

   This phenomenon of *-reru* used in place of *-rareru* is not limited to the verb *miru* alone. In fact, it is becoming so common that it is labeled as *ranuki-kotoba* "*ra*-less words." *Ranuki-kotoba* seems to affect other fairly short, commonly used verbs such as *taberu* and *kuru.*

4.(a) あした八時に来れる (for 来られる)？

   Ashita hachiji ni koreru (or **korareru)?**

   Can you come at 8 tomorrow?

(b) こんな物食べれ (for 食べられ）ないよ。
Konna mono tabere (or taberare)nai yo.
I can't eat things like this.

Teachers of Japanese invariably frown upon this phenomenon, and most Japanese textbooks for foreigners do not include these forms despite their prevalence. The reason *mireru, tabereru,* etc., are often used in place of *mirareru, taberareru,* etc., is because the potential forms and the passive forms being exactly the same could sometimes cause confusion. I am sure those who use *ranuki-kotoba* are instinctively avoiding that. Also, *-reru* versions being shorter and simpler than their *-rareru* counterparts may be contributing to the popularity of *ranuki-kotoba.* My suggestion would be: "Don't hesitate to use *ranuki-kotoba* in the company of young people on informal occasions but, on formal occasions, and especially in the presence of older Japanese or Japanese language teachers, try to avoid the shorter versions. Although I myself avoid their use, *ranuki-kotoba* will probably win out in the long run despite the purists' disapproval.

MISOSHIRU 味噌汁 miso soup

Very often, words denoting items of food vary, depending on whether they are used at home or at restaurants. Miso soup, for example, is usually called *omiotsuke* domestically, but *(o)misoshiru* at restaurants. Likewise, Japanese pickles are most normally called *okooko* or *(o)tsukemono* at home, but *oshinko* at restaurants. Some expressions such as *murasaki* (for *shooyu*) "soy sauce" and *agari* (for *ocha*) "tea" sound so professional that lay people should refrain from using them.

MITAI みたい like (such and such)

Mitai is an informal, colloquial equivalent of *yoo* and can be used wherever the latter is used in the sense of "like." For example,

1.(a) 今度の試験は難しいみたい (or よう) だ。

   Kondo no shiken wa muzukashii mitai (or yoo) da.

   The exam that's coming up sounds like a difficult one.

 (b) 今晩は雪が降るみたい (or よう) だ。

   Konban wa yuki ga furu mitai (or yoo) da.

   It looks like it's going to snow this evening.

One difference in usage between *mitai* and *yoo,* however, is that, after a noun, *yoo* must be preceded by *no,* whereas *mitai* can be attached to a noun directly.

2. あそこに田中さんみたい(or のよう)な人がいる。

   Asoko ni Tanaka-san mitai (or no yoo) na hito ga iru.

   There's a man over there who looks like Mr. Tanaka.

Needless to say, *mitai* cannot be replaced by *yoo* where the latter does not mean "like."

3. 先生にすぐレポートを書くように(＊みたいに)言われた。

   Sensei ni sugu repooto o kaku yoo ni (*mitai ni) iwareta.

   I was told by the teacher to write a report immediately.

Mitai sounds like another *mitai,* which is the stem of *miru* (i.e., *-mi*) plus *tai,* and means "want to see."

4. 桜が／を見たい。

   Sakura ga/o mitai.

   I want to see cherry blossoms.

Since, in informal conversation, particles such as *ga* and *o* are consistently dropped, 4 above without *ga* or *o* would sound and look very much like 5 below.

5. 桜みたい

   sakura mitai

   like cherry blossoms

There are two important differences, however. First, *mitai* meaning "want to see" is usually written 見たい, whereas *mitai* meaning "like" always appears in hiragana, i.e., みたい. Second, the accent is different. 見たい is accented on *ta,* i.e., *mitai,* while みたい is accented on *mi,* i.e., *mitai.* Therefore, *Sakura mitai* would mean "I want to see cherry blossoms," but *Sakura mitai* would mean "That's like cherry blossoms."

MITSUKARU 見つかる **to be found**

Japanese has a large number of intransitive/transitive verb pairs such as *shimaru* ("something closes"); *shimeru* ("to close something"); *aku* ("something opens"); *akeru* ("to open something"), etc. *Mitsukaru* ("something is found") - *mitsukeru* ("to find something") is one of those pairs. What one should note about *mitsukaru* is: there is no single-word English counterpart, and the idea of *mitsukaru* must be expressed in a passive construction. For example,

1. 隠れていたのだが、すぐ見つかってしまった。
   Kakurete ita no da ga, sugu mitsukatte shimatta.
   I was hiding but was discovered right away.

In this situation, one could also express the same English sentence with the passive form of the transitive counterpart *mitsukeru,* as in

2. 隠れていたのだが、すぐ見つけられてしまった。
   Kakurete ita no da ga, sugu mitsukerarete shimatta.

Although the two sentences basically mean the same, most Japanese speakers would probably use 1 rather than 2, preferring to describe the situation as something that happened spontaneously rather than as an action taken by someone.

Another example that might be even more revealing follows:

3. 仕事が見つからなくて (rather than 見つけられなくて) 困っ
   ているんです。

   **Shigoto ga mitsukaranakute (rather than mitsukerare-
   nakute) komatte iru n desu.**

   I'm in trouble, not being able to find a job.

This example makes it even clearer that English prefers to describe a situation from the standpoint of someone doing something whereas Japanese prefers to do the same from the standpoint of something happening.

MITSUKERU 見つける to find (out)

Mitsukeru is, as a rule, used with reference to a concrete object, as in

1. なくしたペンを見つけた。

   Nakushita pen o mitsuketa.

   I found a pen I had lost.

   Mitsukeru is sometimes used about an action, too.

2. 学生がカンニングしているのを見つけた。

   Gakusei ga kanningu shite iru no o mitsuketa.

   I found a student cheating.

This verb, however, is not used about a fact. For example, suppose you were an admirer of President John F. Kennedy. One day you learn that he was quite a womanizer and feel crushed. Use *shiru* rather than *mitsukeru* in that case.

3. ケネディー大統領が女好きだったことを知って (＊見つ
   けて) がっかりした。

   **Kenedii Daitooryoo ga onnazuki datta koto o shitte
   (*mitsukete) gakkari shita.**

   I was disappointed to find out that President Kennedy was a womanizer.

MIYAGE みやげ gift, present

The generic expression for "gift" is *okurimono* lit., "a thing to present someone with."

1. 誰だって贈り物をもらうのは嬉しい。
    Dare datte okurimono o morau no wa ureshii.
    Everyone is happy to receive a gift.

Miyage, or *omiyage,* is a kind of *okurimono,* but its use is limited to two specific occasions. First, it is a gift you buy on a trip to take home to your family or friends.

2. ハワイからおみやげにマカダミア・ナッツを買ってくるよ。
    Hawai kara omiyage ni makadamia nattsu o katte kuru yo.
    I'll buy you guys a gift of macadamia nuts in Hawaii.

Second, *(o)miyage* refers to a gift one takes along when one visits someone.

3. 田中さんのうちへ行く時、チーズのおみやげを持っていこう。
    Tanaka-san no uchi e iku toki, chiizu no omiyage o motte ikoo.
    I think I'll take a gift of cheese when I visit the Tanakas.

In this second sense, *temiyage* 手みやげ (lit., hand-*miyage*) may also be used just to focus on the fact that the gift is being carried by hand.

Because of these restrictions, *(o)miyage* cannot be used for things like Christmas presents.

4. パーティーへ行ったりプレゼント (or 贈り物, but not ＊みやげ) を交換したりするだけが日本のクリスマスです。
    Paatii e ittari purezento (or okurimono, but not miyage) o kookan-shitari suru dake ga Nihon no Kurisumasu desu.
    Japanese Christmas is just going to parties and exchanging gifts.

MOCHIIRU 用いる to use, utilize

Mochiiru is quite similar in meaning to *tsukau,* which also means "to use." In conversation, the latter is the standard form since the former is basically a written expression. Compare 1 and 2.

1. スラングが分からない時は、新しい辞書を使わなきゃ。

    Surangu ga wakaranai toki wa, atarashii jisho o tsukawanakya.

    You've got to use a new dictionary when you don't understand a slang word.

2. スラングが理解できない時は、新しい辞書を用いる必要がある。

    Surangu ga rikai dekinai toki wa, atarashii jisho o mochiiru hitsuyoo ga aru.

    You need to make use of a new dictionary when you fail to comprehend a slang expression.

MOCHIRON もちろん of course

Mochiron means "of course," as in

1. 日本人はもちろんアジア人だ。

    Nihonjin wa mochiron Ajiajin da.

    A Japanese is of course an Asian.

There is an extended use of *mochiron,* which could be translated into English as "let alone," in the sense of "not only."

2. 日本語の学生は、仮名はもちろん漢字も勉強しなければならない。

    Nihongo no gakusei wa, kana wa mochiron kanji mo benkyoo-shinakereba naranai.

    Students of Japanese must study kanji, not to mention kana.

Although this extended use may look a little different, it comes from the idea of "of course they must study kana but, in addition, they must also study kanji." The basic idea for 1 and 2 is therefore virtually the same.

MONKU 文句 word, phrase; complaint, objection

Monku is sometimes used to simply mean "word" or "phrase."

1.(a) 卒業アルバムに何か書くように頼まれたが、いい文句を思いつかなかった。

Sotsugyooarubamu ni nani ka kaku yoo ni tanomareta ga, ii monku o omoitsukanakatta.

I was asked to write something in the graduation album, but I couldn't think of anything worthwhile to say.

(b) 日本語は決まり文句の多い国語だと思う。

Nihongo wa kimarimonku no ooi kokugo da to omou.

I think Japanese is a language with a large number of set phrases.

More commonly, however, *monku* means "complaint," especially in the phrase *monku o iu* "to make a complaint."

2. 文句ばかり言っている人はきらわれる。

Monku bakari itte iru hito wa kirawareru.

A person who complains all the time will be disliked.

MOO もう already

Moo is the opposite of *mada* and is used when a state of being changes, whether it is used in an affirmative or negative sentence.

1.(a) もうおなかがいっぱいだ。

Moo onaka ga ippai da.

I'm already full.

(b) もう何も食べられない。

Moo nani mo taberarenai.

I can't eat any more.

Although the English translation of *moo* comes out quite differently in a negative sentence such as 1(b) above, its basic meaning remains the same, i.e., "I'm already in the state where I can't eat anything."

Moo is colloquially used quite often when a speaker finds himself in a helpless situation or has just seen or heard something highly unpleasant or unbearable. For example, when a mother goes into her child's room and finds it in a total mess, she might mumble to herself:

2. 全くもう！

Mattaku moo!

This literally means "Totally already," i.e., "I'm already aggravated enough. Don't try to shock me any further!" It is similar to the English phrase "Enough already!"

Moo meaning "already" looks the same as another *moo* meaning "more" used with numerals.

3. コーヒーをもう一杯飲んだ。

Koohii o moo ippai nonda.

I drank one more cup of coffee.

This *moo* is accentless whereas *moo* meaning "already" is accented on the first syllable, as in 4 below.

4. コーヒーをもう一杯飲んだ。

Koohii o moo ippai nonda.

I already drank a cup of coffee.

MORAU もらう **to receive**

Although *morau* is usually translated as "to receive," there are many cases where *morau* would be inappropriate. In each of the examples below, the first sentence is wrong and should be replaced by the second.

1.(a) ＊私は花子の愛をもらった。
   ＊Watashi wa Hanako no ai o moratta.
   I received Hanako's love.
 (b) 私は花子の愛を受けた。
   Watashi wa Hanako no ai o uketa.
2.(a) ＊父は癌の手術をもらった。
   ＊Chichi wa gan no shujutsu o moratta.
   My father had a cancer operation.
 (b) 父は癌の手術を受けた。
   Chichi wa gan no shujutsu o uketa.
3.(a) ＊子供たちはテレビから大きな影響をもらう。
   ＊Kodomo-tachi wa terebi kara ookina eikyoo o morau.
   lit., Children receive a huge influence from TV.
 (b) 子供たちはテレビから大きな影響を受ける。
   Kodomo-tachi wa terebi kara ookina eikyoo o ukeru.

   The above examples simply show that with some nouns such as *ai* "love," *shujutsu* "operation," and *eikyoo* "influence," *morau* cannot be used.

MOTTAINAI もったいない **wasteful**

Mottainai is often used as follows:
1. ごはんを食べないで捨てるのはもったいない。
   Gohan o tabenai de suteru no wa mottainai.
   It's wasteful to throw away uneaten rice.

   Mottainai implies that the object wasted is something valuable that should be utilized to the fullest. It often carries a reproachful tone.

   Mottainai is an act or an action, and never a person, whereas English "wasteful" could mean "wasting" and may modify a person, as in "He is a wasteful man." To express the same idea in Japanese, however, one would have to say the following instead:

2.　彼は浪費的な（＊もったいない）男だ。

   Kare wa roohiteki na (*mottainai) otoko da.

   He is a wasteful man.

MOTTO もっと more

Motto may be used with a transitive verb, as in 1, or may modify an adjective or an adverb, as in 2 or 3.

1.　もっと下さい。

   Motto kudasai.

   Please give me more.

2.　もっと安いのはありませんか。

   Motto yasui no wa arimasen ka.

   Aren't there cheaper ones?

3.　もっと速く歩きましょう。

   Motto hayaku arukimashoo.

   Let's walk faster.

   Motto may not be used with a numeral. Use *moo* instead in that case, as in

4.　もう（＊もっと）一つ下さい。

   Moo (*motto) hitotsu kudasai.

   Please give me one more.

   Motto may not be used negatively, as in 5. Use *moo* instead.

5.　もう（＊もっと）食べたくない。

   Moo (*motto) tabetakunai.

   I don't want to eat any more.

MOTTOMO 最も the most

Mottomo is used for superlatives just as *ichiban* is. For example,

1.　富士山は日本で最も(orいちばん)高い山だ。
   Fujisan wa Nihon de mottomo (or ichiban) takai yama da.
   Mt. Fuji is the highest mountain in Japan.

   The difference between *mottomo* and *ichiban* is that the former is a written form and is not suitable for conversation while the latter may be used in most cases. *Mottomo* therefore would sound strange if used with a highly colloquial expression, as in

2.　いちばん(＊最も)たまげたのは誰？
   Ichiban (* mottomo) tamageta no wa dare?
   Who was the one that was the most flabbergasted?

   Ichiban is sometimes followed by *da* to mean "(such and such) is the best thing," but *mottomo* may not be so used, as in

3.　暑い日には、冷たいビールがいちばんだ(＊最もだ)。
   Atsui hi ni wa tsumetai biiru ga ichiban da (*mottomo da).
   On a hot day, nothing surpasses cold beer.

MURI 無理 unreasonable

Once a student of mine who was exasperated about Japanese wrote in a composition, *Nihongo wa muri da* to mean "Japanese is impossible." The sentence should have been either 1(a) or 1(b).

1.(a)　日本語は私には無理だ。
   Nihongo wa watashi ni wa muri da.
   It is unreasonable to expect me to learn Japanese. (i.e., Japanese is impossible for me to learn.)

  (b)　日本語を一、二年でマスターするのは無理だ。
   Nihongo o ichi-ninen de masutaa-suru no wa muri da.
   It's unreasonable to expect to master Japanese in a year or two.

   Muri is often used in the phrase *muri o suru* "to do something to an unreasonable extent, e.g., to work too hard."

2. 無理をすると病気になりますよ。
    Muri o suru to byooki ni narimasu yo.
    If you work unreasonably hard, you'll get sick.

NAGARA ながら while; even though

Nagara is used to express two actions occurring simultaneously. The subject of the two actions must be one and the same.

1. 私はいつも新聞を読みながら朝ご飯を食べる。
    Watashi wa itsumo shinbun o yomi-nagara asagohan o taberu.
    I always eat breakfast while reading the paper.

When the subjects are different, the sentence becomes ungrammatical. In that case, *aida* must be used instead.

2. 私は妻が新聞を読んでいる間 (＊読みながら) 昼寝をしていた。
    Watashi wa tsuma ga shinbun o yonde iru aida (*yomi-nagara) hirune o shite ita.

Nagara has another meaning, i.e., "even though." In this case, too, the same subject must hold for both clauses.

3. ジョンは日本語が下手ながら、いつも一生懸命話そうとする。
    Jon wa Nihongo ga heta nagara, itsumo isshookenmei hanasoo to suru.
    John always tries hard to speak Japanese even though he is not good at it.

The same-subject rule does not apply, however, in the case of some idiomatic expressions, especially *zannen-nagara* "regrettably" (lit., "even though it is regrettable"), as in

4. 残念ながら日本チームは負けてしまった。
    Zannen-nagara, Nihon-chiimu wa makete shimatta.
    Regrettably, the Japanese team lost.

Of these two uses of *nagara,* the first one is far more common, appearing both in speech and writing. The latter use, i.e., "although," is basically a written expression. One of the few exceptions would be *zannen-nagara,* which could be used in speech as a set phrase.

NAKA 中 **in, inside**

English-speaking students of Japanese tend to overuse *naka.* They should remember that *naka,* which means "in," is probably not used as often as English "in." The reason is because Japanese has *ni* and *de,* which, by themselves, can mean "in," as in

1.(a) 太郎は日本に（＊日本のの中に）住んでいる。

Taroo wa Nihon ni (*Nihon no naka ni) sunde iru.

Taro lives in Japan.

(b) 教室で勉強した。

Kyooshitsu de benkyoo-shita.

I studied in the classroom.

Kyooshitsu no naka de would be allowed only if it contrasts with *kyooshitsu no soto de* "outside the classroom," as in

2. A：教室の外で勉強したんですか。

Kyooshitsu no soto de benkyoo-shita n desu ka.

Did you study outside the classroom?

B：いいえ、雨が降っていたので、（教室の）中で勉強したんですよ。

Iie, ame ga futte ita node, (kyooshitsu no) naka de benkyoo-shita n desu yo.

No, I studied in the classroom because it was raining.

To repeat, *naka* "in" is often omitted unless the speaker has a reason to emphasize the idea of "in" in contrast with other location words such as *soto* "outside," *ue* "on top," and *shita* "under."

NAKANAKA なかなか quite, rather

Nakanaka, when used with words of positive meanings, signifies "quite" or "rather."

1. ここのすしはなかなかおいしいですね。

   Koko no sushi wa nakanaka oishii desu ne.

   This restaurant serves pretty good sushi, doesn't it?

   When used this way, *nakanaka* is very much like other intensifiers such as *totemo, taihen,* and *hijoo ni.* The difference, first of all, is that *totemo, taihen,* and *hijoo ni* may be used with words of negative meanings while *nakanaka* may not.

2. (a) この本はとても／大変／非常につまらない。

   Kono hon wa totemo/taihen/hijoo ni tsumaranai.

   This book is very uninteresting.

   (b) ここの料理はとても／大変／非常にまずい。

   Koko no ryoori wa totemo/taihen/hijoo ni mazui.

   This restaurant serves very bad food.

   Second, when *nakanaka* is used with words of positive meanings, it implies, unlike *totemo/taihen/hijoo ni,* that the speaker feels something is better than expected. In that sense, *nakanaka* is similar to *zuibun.*

3. スミスさん、日本語がなかなか／ずいぶん上手になりましたね。

   Sumisu-san, Nihongo ga nakanaka/zuibun joozu ni narimashita ne.

   Mr. Smith, your Japanese has improved a lot!

   There is a slight difference, however, between *nakanaka* and *zuibun,* in that the latter shows a greater surprise than *nakanaka.* Moreover, since *nakanaka* could sound a little condescending, you should probably avoid using it when giving a compliment to a higher-status person.

4. 先生、ずいぶん(?なかなか)テニスがお強いんですね。

   Sensei, zuibun (?nakanaka) tenisu ga otsuyoi n desu ne.

   Professor, you're a very good tennis player, indeed!

Nakanaka . . . nai, on the other hand, means "not easily," as in

5.　日本語は、一年だけの勉強ではなかなか上手になるまい。

Nihongo wa, ichi-nen dake no benkyoo de wa nakanaka joozu ni narumai.

Japanese cannot be easily mastered in just one year.

NAKU 泣く **to cry, weep**

English has a group of verbs that describe different ways tears come out, such as "cry," "weep," "sob," "whimper," and "wail." In Japanese, different types of crying are often expressed by adding onomatopoetic adverbs to the basic verb *naku.*

1.(a)　おいおい泣く

oioi naku

to sob

(b)　めそめそ泣く

mesomeso naku

to whimper

(c)　えーんえーんと泣く

eeneen to naku

to wail

Naku written 鳴く is used for animals making sounds. In Japanese, different sounds made by different animals are expressed by onomatopoetic adverbs while, in English, different verbs are used for sounds made by different animals.

2.(a)　猫はニャーニャー鳴く。

Neko wa nyaanyaa naku.

Cats meow. (lit., cats go *nyaanyaa.*)

(b)　牛はモーモー鳴く。

Ushi wa moomoo naku.

Cows moo. (lit., cows go *moomoo.*)

(c) 烏はカーカー鳴く。

Karasu wa kaakaa naku.

Crows caw. (lit., crows go *kaakaa.*)

(d) 雀はチュンチュン鳴く。

Suzume wa chunchun naku.

Sparrows chirp. (lit., sparrows go *chunchun.*)

NAMAE 名前 **name**

In a broad sense, *namae* may mean either "full name," "family name," or "given name," as in

1. 彼の名前は	(a) 田中太郎	
	(b) 田中	だ。
	(c) 太郎	
Kare no namae wa	**(a) Tanaka Taro**	
	(b) Tanaka	**da.**
	(c) Taroo	
His name is	(a) Taro Tanaka.	
	(b) Tanaka.	
	(c) Taro.	

In a narrow sense, however, *namae* means "given name" only.

2. 彼の苗字は田中で、名前は太郎だ。

Kare no myooji wa Tanaka de, namae wa Taroo da.

His family name is Tanaka, and his given name is Taro.

NAN DA 何だ **What!; Why!**

Nan da ordinarily means "What is it?", as in

1. これは何だ。

Kore wa nan da.

What is this?

Nan da, however, is sometimes used not as an interrogative, but as rather as an exclamation of surprise, disappointment, or disgust. For example, suppose you hear some noise at the door and open it, expecting a visitor, but find only a stray cat. In that case, you are likely to say,

2.　何だ、野良猫か。

Nan da, noraneko ka.

Why, it's a stray cat! (implication: To my disappointment, I find only a stray cat.)

NAN NO HI 何の日 what kind of day

Nan no hi literally looks like "what day," but it does not really mean that. In English, if one asks "What day is today?", it normally means "What day of the week is today?" In Japanese, on the other hand, if you want to know the day of the week, you must ask *Kyoo wa naniyoobi desu ka,* not *Kyoo wa nan no hi desu ka. Kyoo wa nan no hi desu ka* is used only when you are wondering whether today is any special day. Suppose you are walking along the street in Kyoto with a Japanese friend and suddenly see a long procession. You wonder what the procession is commemorating and ask your friend *Kyoo wa nan no hi desu ka,* and your friend would say, for example, *Kyoo wa Gion Matsuri desu yo* ("Today is Gion Festival Day").

NARUBEKU なるべく as (much) as possible; if possible

Narubeku is used as follows, and is usually replaceable by *dekiru dake.*

1.(a) 宿題はなるべく／できるだけ早く やることにしている。

Shukudai wa narubeku/dekiru dake hayaku yaru koto ni shite iru.

I make it a rule to get my homework done as soon as possible.

(b) あしたのパーティーには、なるべく／できるだけ来てくださいね。

Ashita no paatii ni wa, narubeku/dekiru dake kite kudasai ne.

Please come to tomorrow's party if at all possible.

There is a slight difference in connotation between *narubeku* and *dekiru dake,* however. According to *Effective Japanese Usage Guide* (pp. 474–476), *dekiru dake* is more like "to one's utmost ability" and is therefore more emphatic than *narubeku.*

Another difference between the two expressions is that *dekiru dake* may modify a noun by using *no* whereas *narubeku* is not used that way.

2. あなたのためなら、できるだけ(＊なるべく)のことはします。

Anata no tame nara, dekiru dake (*narubeku) no koto wa shimasu.

If it's for you, I'll do the best I can.

NEBOO-SURU 寝坊する to oversleep; to sleep late

In English, one may say "I slept late" to mean "I overslept." American students who come to a morning class late may make the mistake of translating "I slept late" into *Osoku nemashita* to mean "I overslept." They should actually say:

1. 寝坊して遅くなりました。

Neboo-shite osoku narimashita.

I was late because I overslept.

Osoku nemashita has its own meaning, i.e., "I went to bed late," as in

2.　ゆうべ遅く寝たので、けさ早く起きられませんでした。
Yuube osoku neta node, kesa hayaku okiraremasen deshita.
Because I went to bed late last night, I wasn't able to get up early this morning.

NICHIBEI 日米 Japan-U.S.

In English, one normally says "U.S.-Japan relations," "U.S.-Japan Peace Treaty," etc., putting U.S. before Japan. In Japanese, it is the other way around. One must say *Nichibei-kankei* (lit., "Japan-U.S. relations"), *Nichibei-Heiwajooyaku* (lit., "Japan-U.S. Peace Treaty"), etc. It seems that we want to place our countries first in our respective languages.

NIGATE 苦手 weak point

Nigate is similar to *heta.*
1.　私はスキーが苦手だ。
Watashi wa sukii ga nigate/heta da.
I am not good at skiing.

Nigate, however, is not the same as *heta.* Whereas *heta* is an objective description, *nigate* is more subjective. For example, in Sentence 1 above, *nigate* implies that the speaker is not only a poor skier but is not too fond of the sport or is embarrassed to talk about it. If someone is *heta* at skiing, he can still like it. There is even a proverb *Heta no yokozuki* meaning "There are people who are crazy about something without being good at it." On the other hand, if someone is *nigate* at something, he cannot possibly like it; in the above proverb, therefore, *heta* may not be replaced by *nigate.*

Nigate is sometimes used with respect to one's attitude toward someone, as in

2.　私は吉田さんのような人は苦手だ。

Watashi wa Yoshida-san no yoo na hito wa nigate (*heta) da.

I find it hard to deal with someone like Mr. Yoshida.

Nigate used in this sense is naturally not a synonym for *heta.*

NIGIRI 握り **a kind of sushi**

Usually a Japanese noun does not change its meaning whether or not it is preceded by an honorific prefix *o.* For example, *sushi* and *osushi* refer to the same object, the only difference being the *o-* version sounds more polite. With *nigiri,* however, the same cannot be said. *Nigiri* is short for *nigiri-zushi,* i.e., a small oblong chunk of sushi rice topped with a slice of fish. *Onigiri,* on the other hand, refers to a rice ball with things like a pickled plum inside and often covered with *nori,* a sheet of dried black seaweed. If you want to eat *nigiri,* you go to a sushi restaurant but, if you want an *onigiri,* you either make one yourself or go to a Japanese-style non-sushi restaurant.

NIHON 日本 **Japan**

I am sure students of Japanese sometimes wonder about the difference between the two common ways of referring to Japan in Japanese: *Nihon* and *Nippon.*

Before and during World War II, the Japanese government promoted the pronunciation *Nippon* rather than *Nihon.* The reason was apparently that *Nippon* sounds more lively and powerful than *Nihon* because it contains a plosive sound. Japanese athletes representing their country at sporting events such as the Olympics often wear uniforms with *Nippon* printed on them in *romaji,* never *Nihon.* Certainly *Nippon* is better suited to cheering than is *Nihon.* Strangely, however, in daily conversation, *Nihon* seems to be preferred by most speakers of Japanese.

NIHON-SHIKI 日本式 **Japanese-system/style**

Nihon-shiki and *Nihon-fuu* (or *wafuu*) may both be translated "Japanese-style." Their uses overlap somewhat, but not completely.

Nihon-shiki is basically for contraptions, systems, and such, as in
1. 日本式のトイレは、しゃがまなければならない。
    Nihon-shiki no toire wa, shagamanakereba naranai.
    A Japanese-style toilet requires squatting.
    Nihon-fuu (or *wafuu*) *no toire* calls up a different image. It could very well be a Western-style toilet, but the walls may be covered with Japanese wall paper or the window might look shoji-style. In Sentence 1, therefore, *Nihon-fuu* would not be suitable.
2. アメリカの高校には、日本語のクラスを日本式／日本風
    のおじぎで始める所もある。
    Amerika no kookoo ni wa, Nihongo no kurasu o Nihon-shiki/fuu no ojigi de hajimeru tokoro mo aru.
    In some American high schools, Japanese language classes begin with Japanese-style bowing.

In Sentence 2, *Nihon-shiki no ojigi* is a bow that strictly follows the Japanese school tradition whereas *Nihon-fuu no ojigi* could be any bow as long as it is similar to the Japanese bow.

NI KANSHITE に関して concerning

Ni kanshite means "concernng," and is used adverbially only, as in

1. 日米政府代表は、日米貿易に関してはげしい議論をした。

   Nichibei-seifudaihyoo wa, Nichibei-booeki ni kanshite hageshii giron o shita.

   The representatives of the U.S. and Japanese governments vehemently argued about U.S.-Japan trade.

Ni kanshite must be replaced by *ni kansuru* when used adjectivally, modifying a noun. If you wish to use *ni kanshite* adjectivally, you must insert *no* before the following noun, as in

2. 日米政府代表は、日米貿易に関する (or に関しての) 会合を開いた。

   Nichibei-seifudaihyoo wa, Nichibei-booeki ni kansuru (or kanshite no) kaigoo o hiraita.

   The representatives of the U.S. and Japanese governments held a meeting that concerned U.S.-Japan trade.

Ni kanshite is a formal written form and is not used in normal speech. In conversation or less formal written Japanese, *ni tsuite* should be used, as in

3. 先生、アメリカの議会について説明して下さい。

   Sensei, Amerika no gikai ni tsuite setsumei-shite kudasai.

   Professor, please explain the U.S. Congress to us.

NIKU 肉 meat; flesh

In English, "flesh" and "meat" refer to the same object, but meat is used usually when eating is the issue. In Japanese, no such distinction is made.

1. 太郎は大学に入って肉がついてきた。
   Taroo wa daigaku ni haitte niku ga tsuite kita.
   Taro has put on some weight (lit., has gained some flesh) since he entered college.
2. このごろの若い日本人は、魚より肉の方が好きだそうだ。
   Konogoro no wakai Nihonjin wa sakana yori niku no hoo ga suki da soo da.
   I hear young Japanese these days prefer meat to fish.

NINKI 人気 **popularity**

Ninki by itself means "popularity," not "popular." If you wish to say someone or something is popular, therefore, you must say *ninki ga aru* (lit., to have popularity).

1. サッカーは人気がある。
   Sakkaa wa ninki ga aru.
   Soccer is popular.

To say "to become popular," use *ninki ga deru,* not *ninki ni naru.*

2. 日本でサッカーの人気が出た（＊人気になった）のは、数年前だったと思う。
   Nihon de sakkaa no ninki ga deta (*ninki ni natta) no wa suunen mae datta to omou.
   I think it must have been several years ago that soccer became popular in Japan.

Ninki may be attached to other nouns to create compound nouns such as *ninkisakka* "popular novelist."

3. 村上春樹はこのごろ人気作家になった。
   Murakami Haruki wa konogoro ninkisakka ni natta.
   Haruki Murakami has lately become a popular novelist.
   (See also HAYARU and SAKAN.)

NINSHIN-SURU 妊娠する **to become pregnant**

In English, one "becomes pregnant" but, in Japanese, one "does pregnancy."

1. 田中さんは奥さんが妊娠した(＊妊娠になった)そうだ。

   Tanaka-san wa okusan ga ninshin-shita (*ninshin ni natta) soo da.

   I hear Mr. Tanaka's wife is pregnant.

   There are many other expressions in Japanese that do not require *naru* although their English counterparts use "become." For example,

English	Japanese
become angry	*okoru*
become fat	*futoru*
become hungry	*onaka ga suku*
become old	*toshi o toru*
become popular	*ninki ga deru*
become thirsty	*nodo ga kawaku*

NITE-IRU 似ている **to be similar; look alike; resemble**

Nite-iru comes from the dictionary form *niru,* but the latter is rarely used.

1. 韓国語の文法は日本語の文法に似ていると言われる。

   Kankokugo no bunpoo wa Nihongo no bunpoo ni nite iru to iwareru.

   Korean grammar is said to be similar to Japanese grammar.

2. 花子は母親にあまり似ていない。

   Hanako wa hahaoya ni amari nite-inai.

   Hanako does not resemble her mother very much.

As a modifier in prenoun position, either *nite iru* or *nita* may be used, as in

3. 日本には、富士山に似ている／似た山がけっこう多い。

Nihon ni wa, Fujisan ni nite-iru/nita yama ga kekkoo ooi.

In Japan, there are quite a few mountains that look like Mt. Fuji.

NI YORU TO によると **according to**

Ni yoru to means "according to," and is used as follows:

1.(a) 天気予報によると、きょうは雨が降るそうだ。

Tenkiyohoo ni yoru to, kyoo wa ame ga furu soo da.

According to the weather forecast, it's going to rain today.

(b) ブラウンさんによると、シカゴの冬はかなり寒いらしい／ようだ。

Buraun-san ni yoru to, Shikago no fuyu wa kanari samui rashii/yoo da.

According to Mr. Brown, winter in Chicago is pretty cold.

As the above examples show, when *ni yoru to* is used, the sentence normally ends with *soo da, rashii,* or *yoo da* whereas, in English, there is no need for the addition of expressions such as "it seems," "it looks like," or "it sounds like." *Ni yoreba* is synomymous with *ni yoru to* and is used in exactly the same way. *Ni yotte,* however, is different in meaning and must not be confused with *ni yoru to.* Although *ni yotte* is sometimes translated as "according to," it could mean "according to" only in the sense of "in accordance with," as in

2. 悪人は法律によって裁かれるべきだ。

Akunin wa hooritsu ni yotte sabakareru beki da.

Villains should be tried in accordance with the law.

In 1(a) and 1(b), therefore, *ni yotte* cannot replace *ni yoru to*.

(See also NI YOTTE below.)

NI YOTTE によって **depending on; by means of; because of; by**

Ni yotte has different meanings, but the most common is "depending on," as in

1. 日本語のアクセントは地方によってかなり違う。

    Nihongo no akusento wa chihoo ni yotte kanari chigau.

    Japanese accent varies considerably, depending on the region.

    The other uses are mainly for written or formal Japanese. For example, one of the meanings, "by," is used in written passive sentences, as in

2. 日本はアメリカの軍隊によって占領された。

    Nihon wa Amerika no guntai ni yotte senryoo-sareta.

    Japan was occupied by American troops.

    In conversation, *ni yotte* is normally replaced by *ni* alone. Sentence 2, therefore, becomes *Nihon wa Amerika no guntai ni senryoo sareta.*

NOBORU 登る **to climb**

In English, it is perfectly all right to use "climb" as a transitive verb, as in "I climbed Mt. Fuji." In Japanese, on the other hand, climbing Mt. Fuji takes the particle *ni,* not *o.*

1. 富士山に（＊を）登った。

    Fuji-san ni (*o) nobotta.

    I climbed Mt. Fuji.

In certain situations, *o* could be used instead of *ni,* but the connotation would be different.

2.　あの坂をのぼっていく人が見えますか。

Ano saka o nobotte iku hito ga miemasu ka.

Can you see the person going up that slope?

Ni is used when the goal is the main concern while *o* is used when the process is the issue, e.g., in Sentence 1, the speaker is talking about the experience of reaching the top of Mt. Fuji, whereas the speaker of Sentence 2 is talking about someone who is in the process of going uphill.

NOZOMU 望む to hope

In English, "to hope" is a very common verb. If we look up "hope" in an English-Japanese dictionary, we find "corresponding" Japanese verbs such as *nozomu* and *kiboo-suru.* It is true that these Japanese verbs mean "to hope," but they are written expressions not used in speech. For example, how would you say "I hope we'll have good weather tomorrow" in Japanese? The dictionary might suggest *Ashita tenki ga ii koto o nozomimasu,* which is the direct translation of the English. But no one would say that in daily conversation. More normally, one would use an entirely different structure such as

1.(a)　明日いい天気だといいなあ。

Ashita ii tenki da to ii naa.

lit., It'll be nice if the weather is good tomorrow.

(b)　明日いい天気だといいですね。

Ashita ii tenki da to ii desu ne.

lit., It'll be nice if the weather is good tomorrow, won't it?

In other words, instead of directly saying "I hope . . .," Japanese speakers normally say the equivalent of "It'll be nice if . . ." in conversation. "I hope so" does not become

Soo nozomimasu, but rather *Soo da to ii desu ne* (lit., It'll be nice if it's so.").

OCHA O IRERU お茶を入れる to make tea

"Make tea" is not *ocha o tsukuru,* but *ocha o ireru.*
1. 濃いお茶を一杯入れて（＊作って）ください。
    Koi ocha o ippai irete (*tsukutte) kudasai.
    Please make me a strong cup of tea.
    Ocha o tsukuru would mean "to grow tea," as in *Shizuoka-ken ni wa ocha o tsukutte-iru nooka ga ooi* "In Shizuoka Prefecture, there are lots of farmers who cultivate tea."
    The intransitive counterpart of *ireru* is *hairu,* and it is used just as often when talking about making tea, as in
2. お茶が入りましたからどうぞ。
    Ocha ga hairimashita kara doozo.
    Tea is ready (lit., Tea has been made). Please have some.
    Although it is possible to say *Ocha o iremashita* (lit., "I just made tea"), Japanese speakers often prefer the intransitive version, treating the occasion as something that just happened rather than as something they themselves brought about. This is true with many other transitive-intransitive verbs, as well. (See Alfonso, p.885.)

OKAZU おかず food to eat with rice

If you look up *okazu* in a Japanese-English dictionary, you find strange explanations such as "subsidiary articles of diet" and "an accompanying dish." The reason is because there is no equivalent idea in English-speaking cultures and therefore no exact English translation. A typical Japanese dinner always includes rice as the staple, and that is why rice is called *shushoku* (lit., "main food") in Japanese. Along with rice, one may have vegetables, fish, or meat. Those non-rice items are what is called *okazu*. In a typical Japanese family, the following conversation often takes place in the late afternoon between a child who just got home from school and his/her mother, who is preparing dinner:

1. Child: 今晩のおかずなーに。
   Konban no okazu naani.
   lit., What's this evening's *okazu?*
   Mother: テンプラよ。
   Tenpura yo.
   It's tempura.

In normal English, one might just ask "What's today's dinner?" because what is *okazu* to a Japanese is actually conceived of as dinner itself by English speakers for, in English-speaking cultures, bread, which is considered to play the same role as rice, is in truth just something that goes with the main course, not vice versa.

OKONAU 行なう **to do, conduct, carry out, administer**

Okonau "to do" is a synonym for *suru* but is much more formal and, as a rule, used in writing only. When used in speech, it is restricted to formal occasions such as announcements and speeches.

1. 二月十五日に入学試験を行なう。
   Nigatsu juugonichi ni nyuugakushiken o okonau.
   We shall hold an entrance examination on February 15.
   More informally, one would say
2. 二月十五日に入学試験をします。
   Nigatsu juugonichi ni nyuugakushiken o shimasu.
   We'll give an entrance exam on February 15.

Because of its nature, *okonau* is most likely used with nouns denoting formal events and functions, and not with colloquial expressions. In Sentence 3 below, *okonau* would be out of place because *minna de* and *kakekko* are colloquial expressions.

3. みんなでかけっこをする(＊行なう)よ。

    Minna de kakekko o suru (*okonau) yo.

    We're having a foot race for everyone.

Okonau would sound fine, however, if used with formal words describing the same event, as in

4. 全員で徒競走を行ないます。

    Zen'in de tokyoosoo o okonaimasu.

    We shall hold a foot race for everyone.

Since *zen'in de* and *tokyoosoo* are more formal expressions, the whole tone of the sentence allows the use of *okonaimasu* in this case.

The passive form of *okonau*, i.e., *okonawareru*, is often used, although also restricted to formal speech or writing, to mean that "something is a common practice," as in

5. 現代の日本の若者の間には、茶髪という変な習慣が行なわれている。

    Gendai no Nihon no wakamono no aida ni wa, chapatsu to iu hen na shuukan ga okonawarete iru.

    Among today's Japanese youth, a fad called *chapatsu* (i.e., hair dyed brown) has become a common practice.

Okonawareru is not normally replaceable by the passive form of *suru*, i.e., *sareru*.

OKORU 怒る **to become angry; to scold**

There is no adjective in Japanese that means "angry." Japanese has a verb *okoru*, which by itself means "become angry." Don't therefore say *okoru ni naru or *okotte ni naru. Just use *okoru* without *naru*, as in

1.　山本さんはよく怒る。
   Yamamoto-san wa yoku okoru.
   Mr. Yamamoto gets angry often.

To express the idea of "be angry," rather than "become angry," use the *te-iru* form of *okoru,* as in Sentence 2 below.

2.　山本さんはとても怒っている。
   Yamamoto-san wa totemo okotte iru.
   Mr. Yamamoto is very angry.

English speakers may describe their own anger by saying, "I'm angry!!" Don't translate this, however, directly into Japanese by saying *Watashi wa okotte-iru* because *okoru,* as a rule, is not used in reference to the speaker. Instead say something like 3(a) or 3(b).

3.(a)　腹が立つなあ！
   Hara ga tatsu naa!
   I'm boiling inside!

 (b)　しゃくにさわるなあ！
   Shaku ni sawaru naa!
   (lit., something is irritating my temper!)

Okoru is sometimes used as a synonym for *shikaru* in the sense of "to scold." There are, however, two main differences. First, *shikaru* takes the particle *o* whereas *okoru,* when used to mean "to scold," takes *ni.*

4.　日本の教師はよく生徒 ┃ に怒る。
   　　　　　　　　　　　┃ を叱る。

   Nihon no kyooshi wa yoku seito ┃ ni okoru.
   　　　　　　　　　　　　　　　　┃ **shikaru.**
   Japanese teachers often scold their students.

Second, *okoru* means "to scold angrily," while *shikaru* can refer to all manners of scolding including scolding gently and tenderly. In Sentence 3, therefore, *shikaru* is correct, but *okoru* is not.

3. 親は、時には子をやさしく叱る(＊怒る)ことも必要だ。

   Oya wa, toki ni wa ko o yasashiku shikaru (*okoru) koto mo hitsuyoo da.

   It is sometimes necessary for parents to scold their children gently.

⌈OMOIKOMU⌉ 思い込む **to be under the wrong impression**

Omoikomu is to hold an incorrect belief.

1. アメリカ人には日本語が覚えられないと思い込んでいる日本人が多い。

   Amerikajin ni wa Nihongo ga oboerarenai to omoikonde iru Nihonjin ga ooi.

   There are a lot of Japanese who are under the erroneous impression that Americans cannot learn Japanese.

   Shinjikomu is quite similar to *omoikomu* and may be used in Sentence 1 above. *Kangaekomu,* however, is not a synonym for *omoikomu* despite the fact that *omou* and *kangaeru* are synonyms (See *JWTU1*). *Kangaekomu* means "to be deep in thought," as in

2. 先生は学生に難しい質問をされて考え込んで(＊思い込んで)しまった。

   Sensei wa gakusei ni muzukashii shitsumon o sarete kangaekonde (*omoikonde) shimatta.

   The teacher sank deep in thought when he was asked a difficult question by a student.

⌈OMOU⌉ 思う **to think**

One very common error made by students of Japanese is to use a *desu/masu* form before *to omoimasu,* as in 1(a) and 1(b).

1.(a) ＊そうですと思います。
   *Soo desu to omoimasu.
   I think that's the case.

 (b) ＊今日は雨が降りませんと思います。
   *Kyoo wa ame ga furimasen to omoimasu.
   I don't think it'll rain today.

Before *to omoimasu,* always use a plain form. Sentence 1(a) should be *Soo da to omoimasu,* and 1(b) should be *Kyoo wa ame ga furanai to omoimasu.* The reason so many students make these errors when talking to a higher-status person such as their teacher, is that they erroneously believe they can make the whole statement more polite by using a *desu/masu* form before *to omoimasu.* They must remember that the clause preceding *to omoimasu* represents what the speaker is thinking. One's thought is basically what one says to oneself, i.e., it is like a monologue. One need not be formal when speaking to oneself. Hence, no *desu/masu* form before *to omoimasu.*

Other verbs of thinking behave the same way. Never use *desu/masu* before such expressions as *to kangaemasu* "I think," *to soozoo shimasu* "I imagine," etc., even though those verbs themselves may be in the *-masu* form.

Now, observe 1(b) again. The English translation makes the main verb "think" negative, i.e., "I don't think it'll rain today." Note the correct Japanese version is not **Kyoo wa ame ga furu to omoimasen,* but *Kyoo wa ame ga furanai to omoimasu,* making the verb *furu,* rather than *omou,* negative.

Another mistake involving *omou* may occur when a student who has just seen a film or read a book is asked by a Japanese person, *Doo deshita ka?* ("How was it?"). The answer often comes out as **Omoshirokatta to omoimashita,* using two *-ta* forms because of the incorrect association with the English "I thought it was fun," which uses two past tense forms. Say *Omoshiroi to omoimashita* instead because *Omoshirokatta to omoimashita* literally means "I thought it had been fun."

O̅OKI̅I 大きい big; large

Although *ookii* means "big/large," it does not follow that *ookii* can modify any nouns that its English counterparts can. For example, *ookii* does not modify *shokuji* "meal" or any kind of meal such as *asagohan* ("breakfast"), *hirugohan* ("lunch"), or *bangohan* ("dinner"). For example,

1.   ＊大きい朝ご飯を食べた。
     *Ookii asagohan o tabeta.
     I had a big breakfast.

To make the above Japanese acceptable, one would have to say *Asagohan ni takusan tabeta* (lit., "I ate a lot for breakfast.").

For weather-related words such as *ame* ("rain"), *kaze* ("wind"), *yuki* ("snow"), etc., use compounds with the prefix *oo-* (大), rather than use the full adjective *ookii,* as in

2.(a) 大雨　（＊大きい雨）
       ooame (*ookii ame)
       a big rainfall

  (b) 大風　（＊大きい風）
       ookaze (*ookii kaze)
       a big wind

  (c) 大雪　（＊大きい雪）
       ooyuki (*ookii yuki)
       a big snowfall

  (See also OOKII, *JWTU1*).

OSHII 惜しい regrettable; disappointingly close

Oshii has two basic uses. First, it is used in a situation when something comes very close to being achieved but fails to do so, as in

1. 惜しいところで負けてしまった。
   Oshii tokoro de makete shimatta.
   I lost after coming very close to winning.

Second, it is used when something or someone very precious is lost, as in

2. 惜しい人をなくした。
   Oshii hito o nakushita.
   It is regrettable that we lost such a precious person.

OYOGU 泳ぐ to swim

The most common verb for "swimming" is *oyogu.*

1. 今日は暑いからプールへ泳ぎに行こう。
   Kyoo wa atsui kara puuru e oyogi ni ikoo.
   It's so hot today. Let's go swimming in the pool.

Another word for "swimming" is *suiei,* but it is mostly used as a noun. *Suiei-suru* might be found in dictionaries, but it is actually rarely used. "I'm not good at swimming" can be said in two different ways, as in 2(a) and 2(b).

2.(a) 僕は水泳が下手だ。
   Boku wa suiei ga heta da.
   (b) 僕は泳ぐのが下手だ。
   Boku wa oyogu no ga heta da.

When the sport of swimming is meant, *suiei* is the only word used, as in

3. トムは泳ぐのが上手なので、高校の水泳チームに入った。
   Tomu wa oyogu no ga joozu na node, kookoo no suiei-chiimu ni haitta.
   Tom joined his high school's swimming team since he was a good swimmer.

Incidentally, as the English translation for Sentence 3 indicates, it is quite common in English to say "He is a good swimmer instead of "He is good at swimming." In Japanese, on the other hand, the counterpart of the latter is the norm. For example,

4. English: Betty is a wonderful singer.
    Japanese: ベティーは歌がすばらしく上手だ。
               Betii wa uta ga subarashiku joozu da.
               (lit., Betty is good at singing.)

In 4 above, it is possible to say in Japanese *Betii wa subarashii shinga da,* which is the exact translation of "Betty is a wonderful singer." *Betii wa subarashii shinga da* would be possible only in reference to a professional or professional-level singer. It won't be used to describe an amateur who happens to sing well.

RAKU 楽 easy; comfortable

Whereas *yasashii* "easy" is the opposite of *muzukashii* "difficult," *raku* is the opposite of *tsurai* (See TSURAI). *Yasashii* focuses on the lower degree of difficulty, while *raku* stresses the comfortable ease with which something can be handled. For example,

1. アメリカ人の中には、昔の方が暮らしが楽だったという人がいる。

    Amerikajin no naka ni wa, mukashi no hoo ga kurashi ga raku datta to iu hito ga iru.

    There are some Americans who say life used to be easier before.

If you compare 2(a) and 2(b) below, both of which mean "It was an easy job," the difference between *yasashii* and *raku* should become clear.

2.(a) やさしい仕事だった。
       Yasashii shigoto datta.

  (b) 楽な仕事だった。
       Raku na shigoto datta.

In 2(a), the focus is on the fact that the job was not difficult, i.e., the degree of difficulty was very low. In 2(b), on the other hand, the focus is on the fact that the job was handled comfortably and that no exertion was necessary, though the degree of difficulty may, in fact, have been high.

RENSHUU 練習 practice, training, exercise

Renshuu is most typically used as follows:

1. 漢字は何度も書く練習をしないと覚えられない。

   Kanji wa nando mo kaku renshuu o shinai to oboerarenai.

   Kanji can't be learned unless you practice writing them over and over.

In a Japanese-English dictionary, one of the translations given for *renshuu* could be "exercise," but *renshuu* means "exercise" only in the sense of "task for practicing/training," not in the sense of "physical exercise for the sake of health." Sentence 2 below is correct, but Sentence 3 is not.

2. 練習問題のない文法の教科書は、あまり役に立たない。

   Renshuumondai no nai bunpoo no kyookasho wa amari yaku ni tatanai.

   Grammar textbooks without exercises (lit., practice problems) are not very useful.

3. ＊毎日練習するのは体によい。

   ***Mainichi renshuu-suru no wa karada ni yoi.**

   It's good for your health to exercise every day.

For Sentence 3, *renshuu-suru* must be replaced by *undoo-suru.*

RIKA 理科 science

Rika, meaning "science," is used as the name of a subject in elementary through high school covering a broad spectrum including biology, chemistry, and physics.

1. 次郎は高校で英語は出来たが理科は駄目だった。

   Jiroo wa kookoo de Eigo wa dekita ga rika wa dame datta.

   Jiro was good in English but not in science in high school.

When one talks about science in general, apart from school curricula, one must use the term *kagaku,* not *rika.*

2. 科学(＊理科)の進歩は、とどまるところを知らない。

   Kagaku (*rika) no shinpo wa todomaru tokoro o shiranai.

   The progress of science is never-ending.

(See also KAGAGU.)

ROKU NI ろくに hardly; not well; not enough

Roku ni is often translated as "hardly." Don't forget, however, that *roku ni* is regularly accompanied by a negative expression (i.e., *-nai*) unlike "hardly," which is by itself negative and is not accompanied by another negative word.

1. 弘はろくに授業に出ない。

   Hiroshi wa roku ni jugyoo ni denai.

   Hiroshi hardly ever goes to class.

From this example alone, *roku ni* might be considered synonymous with *metta ni* "rarely," as in

2. 弘はめったに授業に出ない。

   Hiroshi wa metta ni jugyoo ni denai.

   Hiroshi rarely goes to class.

There are differences between *roku ni* and *metta ni,* however. First, *metta ni* is objective while *roku ni* is subjective and evaluative. In Sentence 1 above, the speaker is indicating that it is undesirable that Hiroshi does not attend class often enough, whereas, in Sentence 2, the speaker is merely reporting the infrequency of Hiroshi's attendance. Second, while *metta ni* is a frequency word, *roku ni* is a degree word. In Sentence 3 below, therefore, only *roku ni* would be acceptable.

3.　私はスペインのことはろくに(*めったに)知らない。

Watashi wa Supein no koto wa roku ni (*metta ni) shiranai.

I hardly know anything about Spain.

Roku ni is different not only from *metta ni,* but from "hardly," as well, in that the latter is not evaluative. In 3 above, the English is a mere reporting of the fact while the Japanese version implies that the speaker feels embarrassed or humiliated about the fact.

ROONIN 浪人 masterless samurai; high school graduate not yet in college

Roonin originally meant "masterless samurai." We often see those tough guys in samurai movies such as some famous Kurosawa films.

Students who graduate from high school but fail to get into college are somewhat like "masterless samurai" in that they have no place to belong to. They have thus come to be called *roonin,* as in

1.　孝は今浪人中で、予備校で勉強しています。

Takashi wa ima roonin-chuu de, yobikoo de benkyoo-shite imasu.

Takashi is a ronin now studying at a cram school.

High school graduates who spend one year as *roonin* are called *ichinen-roonin,* or *ichiroo* for short. Those who spend two years in that status are, as you might easily guess, *ninen-roonin,* or *niroo.*

RYOOHOO 両方 **both**

Ryoohoo, meaning "both," is mostly used for non-human objects. Very often it is accompanied by *-tomo.*

1. A: すしとテンプラとどっちが好きですか。
   Sushi to tenpura to dotchi ga suki desu ka.
   Which do you like better, sushi or tempura?
   B: 両方(とも)好きです。
   Ryoohoo(-tomo) suki desu.
   I like them both.

2. A: 貴の花と若の花とどっちが好きですか。
   Takanohana to Wakanohana to dotchi ga suki desu ka.
   Whom do you like better, Takanohana or Wakanohana?
   B: 両方(とも)好きです。
   Ryoohoo(-tomo) suki desu.
   I like them both.

Although what 2B says is not entirely wrong, it is probably more natural to use *futari-tomo* (*-tomo* in this case being obligatory) in reference to two persons. *Dotchi mo* or *dochira mo* would also be correct whether what is being talked about is human or non-human.

SABISHII 淋しい／寂しい **lonely, lonesome**

Sabishii means "lonely" but only with regard to the speaker.

1. 母が死んで淋しくなった。
   Haha ga shinde sabishiku natta.
   I am lonely now that my mother is dead. (i.e., I miss my mother now that she is dead.)

As is the case with other adjectives of feelings such as *kanashii* "sad," and *ureshii* "glad," *sabishii* must be used with *-garu, -soo, -yoo, -rashii,* etc., when the subject is someone other than the speaker.

2.(a) 田中さんはガールフレンドが旅行中なので、寂しがっ
ている。

Tanaka-san wa, gaarufurendo ga ryokoo-chuu na node, sabishigatte iru.

Mr. Tanaka is feeling lonely (lit., is showing signs of being lonely) becase his girlfriend has gone on a trip.

(b) 田中さんは寂しそうだ。

Tanaka-san wa sabishi-soo da.

Mr. Tanaks looks lonely.

Sabishii can be used with reference to such things as places, too, as in

3. ここはずいぶん寂しい町だ。

Koko wa zuibun sabishii machi da.

This is a very lonesome town.

In idiomatic Japanese, *sabishii* is sometimes almost synonymous with *kanashii* "sad," but the implication is that the speaker misses something.

4. 和服姿の女性が消えていくのは寂しい。

Wafukusugata no josei ga kieteiku no wa sabishii.

I am sad kimono-clad women are gradually disappearing. (i.e., I miss those kimono-clad women.)

Sabishii appears in some interesting expressions such as *futokoro ga sabishii* "I have little money at the moment" (lit., "My pocket is lonely") and *kuchi ga sabishii* (or *kuchisabishii*) "I'd like to put some food in my mouth" (lit., "My mouth is lonely"). *Sabishii* has another version, i.e., *samishii.*

SAGASU さがす **to look for**

Don't confuse *sagasu* "to look for" with *mitsukeru* "to find." For example, in the following sentence, looking for a job is not difficult. What is difficult is finding a job.

1. 私は大学を卒業しても仕事を見つける(＊さがす)のは難しいだろうと思う。

   Watashi wa daigaku o sotsugyoo-shite mo shigoto o mitsukeru (*sagasu) no wa muzukashii daroo to omou.

   I'm afraid it'll be difficult to find (*look for) a job even if I graduate from college.

Sagasu is for concrete things, not for abstract things such as happiness and peace. For those things, use *motomeru* "to seek."

2. 多くの人が　幸福　を　＊さがしている。
   　　　　　　平和　　求めて

   Ooku no hito ga　koofuku　o　*sagashite iru
   　　　　　　　　　heiwa　　　　motomete

   A lot of people are seeking happiness/peace.

SAIKIN 最近 recently; lately

Saikin may be used in reference to either (a) a current state that has continued since a recent point of time, as in Sentence 1, or (b) an event that occurred at a recent point of time, as in Sentence 2.

1. 日本語は最近外来語が多すぎる。

   Nihongo wa saikin gairaigo ga oosugiru.

   Recently too many loanwords are used in Japanese.

2. 鈴木さんは最近本を出した。

   Suzuki-san wa saikin hon o dashita.

   Mr. Suzuki recently published a book.

Saikin used in the sense of Sentence 1 may be replaced by *konogoro,* as in

3. 日本語はこのごろ外来語が多すぎる。

   Nihongo wa konogoro gairaigo ga oosugiru.

   Recently too many loanwords are used in Japanese.

Saikin in the sense of Sentence 2, however, may not be replaced by *konogoro.*

4.　＊鈴木さんはこのごろ本を出した。

　　*Suzuki-san wa konogoro hon o dashita.

In other words, *konogoro* may not be used in reference to a single action. It may be used, however, if the action repeats itself over a sustained period of time, as in

5.　鈴木さんはこのごろよく本を出す。

　　Suzuki-san wa konogoro yoku hon o dasu.

　　Nowadays Mr. Suzuki often publishes books.

According to Morita (p.160, Vol. 2), the time span covered by *saikin* is much longer than that covered by *konogoro.* Thus, in Sentence 6 below, *saikin* is fine, but *konogoro* probably is not.

6.　日本人が洋服を着るようになったのは、日本の長い歴史
　　から見れば最近(?このごろ)のことだ。

　　Nihonjin ga yoofuku o kiru yoo ni natta no wa, Nihon no nagai rekishi kara mireba saikin (?konogoro) no koto da.

　　In terms of Japan's long history, it was only recently that the Japanese started wearing Western clothes.

What is important about *saikin* is that it means "recent" or "recently" as viewed from the present, and never from a point of time in the past, and there it clearly differs from English "recent." In English, for example, Sentence 7 is correct.

7.　When I visited Mr. Suzuki ten years ago, he gave me a book he had recently published.

In this sentence, "recently" means "a little while before," not "a little while ago." *Saikin,* on the other hand, cannot be used to mean "a little while before" and must be replaced by such expressions as *chotto mae ni,* as in

8. 十年前に鈴木さんを訪ねたら、ちょっと前に（＊最近）出した本をくれた。

   Juunen mae ni Suzuki-san o tazunetara, chotto mae ni (*saikin) dashita hon o kureta.

   When I visited Mr. Suzuki ten years ago, he gave me a book he had recently published.

SAKAN 盛ん prosperous, thriving

Sakan is basically for something that is prospering or thriving, as in

1. 日本で一番盛んなスポーツは野球だろう。

   Nihon de ichiban sakan na supootsu wa yakyuu daroo.

   The most thriving sport in Japan is probably baseball.

   In this sense, *sakan* is quite similar to *ninki ga aru,* which also could be used in Sentence 1. There is, however, a slight difference between them in connotation. *Sakan* implies "strong businesswise," while *ninki ga aru* simply means "popular with a lot of people." See 2(a) and 2(b) below.

2.(a) 日本の造船業は、昔ほど盛んではない。

   Nihon no zoosengyoo wa mukashi hodo sakan de wa nai.

   The Japanese ship-building industry is not as thriving as before.

   (b) 日本の造船業は昔ほど人気がない。

   Nihon no zoosengyoo wa mukashi hodo ninki ga nai.

   The Japaense ship-building industry is not as popular as before.

   2(a) means ship-building in Japan is not as strong as before, while 2(b) means high school or college graduates in Japan do not wish to go into the ship-building business as eagerly as before.

In some cases, *sakan* simply cannot be replaced by *ninki ga aru.* For example,

3. 戦前のアメリカでは、人種差別が盛んだった(＊人気があった)。

   Senzen no Amerika de wa, jinshusabetsu ga sakan datta (*ninki ga atta).

   In pre-war America, racial discrimination was rampant.
   (See also HAYARU and NINKI.)

SAKUNEN 昨年 last year

The most common word for last year is *kyonen,* which is used commonly both in speech and writing. When one wishes to be very formal, however, one may switch to *sakunen.* There is no difference in meaning, only in the degree of formality. See the following pairs of expressions referring to years.

	Normal	Formal
the year before last	*ototoshi*	*issakunen*
last year	*kyonen*	*sakunen*
this year	*kotoshi*	*konnen/honnen*
next year	*rainen*	*myoonen*
the year after next	*sarainen*	*myoogonen*

SAMAZAMA 様々／さまざま various

The most common word for "various" is *iroiro. Samazama,* a more formal expression, could be used almost synonymously. In 1 below, for example, both would be correct.

1. 日本にはいろいろ／さまざまな方言がある。

   Nihon ni wa iroiro/samazama na hoogen ga aru.

   In Japan, there are various kinds of dialects.

There is, however, a slight difference between these two words. *Iroiro* means "many different kinds," and sometimes "many" is emphasized over "different," as in

2.　いろいろ有難うございました。

Iroiro arigatoo gozaimashita.

Thank you for the many (different) things you did for me.

This use of *iroiro* cannot be replaced by *samazama,* which always focuses on "different" rather than "many." That is why *iroiro* and *samazama* can even be used together, as in

3.　日本にはいろいろさまざまな方言がある。

Nihon ni wa iroiro samazama na hoogen ga aru.

In Japan, there are many different kinds of dialects.

SEICHOO-SURU 成長する **to grow**

English "grow" may refer not only to the growth of persons, animals, plants, and inanimate objects, but also to an increase in the number of something. *Seichoo-suru,* on the other hand, may never refer to an increase in the number of something. The use of *seichoo-suru* is therefore correct in Sentences 1 and 2 below, but not in Sentence 3.

1.　子供は十代に急激に成長する。

Kodomo wa juudai ni kyuugeki ni seichoo-suru.

Children grow rapidly in their teens.

2.　日本経済は60年代から70年代にかけて大きく成長した。

Nihonkeizai wa 60-nendai kara 70-nendai ni kakete ook-iku seichoo-shita.

The Japanese economy grew markedly during the 1960s and the 1970s.

3. ＊１９８０年代にアメリカの日本語の学生数はずいぶ
ん増えた（＊成長した）。
***Senkyuuhyakuhachijuu-nendai ni Amerika no Nihongo
no gakuseisuu wa zuibun fueta (*seichoo-shita).**
In the 1980's, the number of Japanese language students
in America grew a lot.

In Sentence 3 above, "to grow in number" should be
fueru.

Seichoo-suru, unlike "grow," is basically a written expression. Sentence 1 above, for example, should be rephrased in
speech as follows:
4. 子供は十代ですごく大きくなる／背が伸びる。
Kodomo wa juudai de sugoku ookiku naru/se ga nobiru.
Children grow a lot taller in their teens.

SEIFU 政府 **government**

English speakers often make the following error in Japanese:
1. ＊あの人は政府に勤めています。
*Ano hito wa seifu ni tsutomete imasu.
That person works for the government.

In 1 above, the English version is of course correct, but
the Japanese, its direct translation, is not. Japanese has
other ways of expressing the same idea, as in 2(a) and 2(b).
2.(a) あの人は官庁に勤めています。
Ano hito wa kanchoo ni tsutomete imasu.
That person works for a government office.
 (b) あの人は官吏／公務員です。
Ano hito wa kanri/koomuin desu.
That person is a government employee.

Also, Japanese speakers normally would prefer being
more specific, e.g.,

3.　あの人は文部省（大蔵省、外務省・・・）に勤めています。

Ano hito wa Monbushoo (Ookurashoo, Gaimushoo ...) ni tsutomete imasu.

That person works for the Ministry of Education (Finance, Foreign Affairs, etc.).

(See also SEIFU in *JWTU1*.)

SEIKATSU 生活 life

Seikatsu, inochi, and *jinsei* are all translated as "life," but each is different. *Seikatsu* means "life" in the sense of "making a living."

1.　物価が高いと生活（＊命、＊人生）が苦しくなる。

Bukka ga takai to seikatsu (*inochi, *jinsei) ga kurushiku naru.

When prices are high, life (i.e., making a living) becomes tough.

Inochi is what sustains life within living things, as in

2.　伊藤さんはまだ若いのに結核で命（＊生活、＊人生）を落とした。

Itoo-san wa mada wakai noni kekkaku de inochi (*seikatsu, *jinsei) o otoshita.

Mr. Ito lost (lit., dropped) his life because of TB despite his young age.

Jinsei is human existence in the sense of "a course of life," as in

3.(a)　人生（＊生活、＊命）は四十からと言われてきた。

Jinsei (*seikatsu, *inochi) wa yonjuu kara to iwarete kita.

It has always been said that life begins at forty.

(b)　彼の人生（＊命）はみじめだった。

Kare no jinsei (*inochi) wa mijime datta.

His life was miserable.

In 3(b) above, *jinsei* may be replaced by *seikatsu,* but the meaning of the sentence would change. 3(b) means "His life from beginning to end was a miserable one," i.e., "he was never happy throughout his life." On the other hand, *Kare no seikatsu wa mijime datta* would seem to focus on a particular period of his life. For example, he grew up happily in the country, but then he moved to Tokyo to enter college and, while there, he had no money and had to live a very sad life.

SEIZEI せいぜい **at the most**

Seizei means "at the most," as in
1. 私はビールを飲んでもせいぜい一杯だ。
    Watashi wa biiru o nonde mo, seizei ippai da.
    I can drink only one glass of beer at the most.
    The implication in the above case is "even if I put in all my effort."
2. 彼の年収はせいぜい二万ドルだろう。
    Kare no nenshuu wa seizei nimandoru daroo.
    His annual income must be at the most $20,000.
    In Sentence 2, *seizei* could imply either "even with his best effort" or "even if I'm trying to give it the highest possible estimate."

SEKAI 世界 **world**

If you look up "world" in an English-Japanese dictionary, you will find at least three words: *sekai, yononaka,* and *seken. Sekai* in a broad sense is the physical world that spreads all over the globe, as in
1. 世界(＊世の中、＊世間)中を旅行してみたい。
    Sekai(*yononaka, *seken)-juu o ryokoo-shite mitai.
    I'd like to travel all over the world.

Sekai in a much narrower sense may refer to a particular segment of society, as in

2. 学者の世界(＊世の中、＊世間)は、いいことばかりではない。

   Gakusha no sekai (*yononaka, *seken) wa, ii koto bakari de wa nai.

   The world of academics is not all pleasant.

Yononaka means "this general world where we live," but not the kind of geographical world consisting of almost 200 countries. For example,

3. 歳を取ると世の中(＊世界、世間)がいやになる人がいる。

   Toshi o toru to yononaka (*sekai, *seken) ga iyani naru hito ga iru.

   Some people, as they grow old, become tired of the world (not in the sense of international politics or anything like that, but rather in terms of what happens around them in daily life in general).

Seken is very close to yononaka but much narrower in scope.

4. こんなことをすると、世間(＊世界、世の中)に対して恥ずかしい。

   Konna koto o suru to, seken (*sekai, *yononaka) ni taishite hazukashii.

   If I do something like this, I'll be too embarrassed to face the world (i.e., the people around me).

SENSHU 選手 a player (selected to play a sport)

Senshu is often translated as "player," but one must be careful not to equate the two. First, a "player" can be a player of anything, e.g., a tennis player, a chess player, a piano player, etc., while *senshu* normally refers only to athletes. Second, a *senshu* is someone selected to play a certain sport while a player can be anyone who plays something. See the difference between 1(a) and 1(b).

1.(a) 太郎はテニスの選手だ。

Taroo wa tenisu no senshu da.

Taro is a varsity tennis player.

(b) ジョンはテニスをする。

Jon wa tenisu o suru.

John is a tennis player.

Sentence 1(a) means "Taro is a member of his school's tennis team" whereas 2(b) is just another way of saying "John plays tennis."

SENZO 先祖 ancestor

There are two main words in Japanese meaning "ancestor": *senzo* and *sosen. Senzo* sounds more personal and usually refers to one's own family ancestors, especially fairly recent (i.e., going back only a few generations). For example, a *butsudan* "family Buddhist altar" is dedicated to one's *senzo,* or more politely, *gosenzo-sama* "dear ancestors," i.e., one's deceased parents, grandparents, and perhaps great grandparents. *Sosen* is a more impersonal term; thus there is no such expression as **gososen-sama* to refer to one's own "dear" ancestors. *Sosen* connotes going back much farther and is therefore preferred to *senzo* when, for example, one talks about the ancestors of the Japanese race, as in

1. 日本人の祖先（？先祖）がどこから来たかということは、今でも時々問題にされる。

Nihonjin no sosen (?senzo) ga doko kara kita ka to iu koto wa, ima demo tokidoki mondai ni sareru.

Where the ancestors of the Japanese race originally came from is still argued about at times.

SHIBARAKUBURI しばらくぶり **for the first time after a long while**

Shibaraku and *shibarakuburi* are often confused by students of Japanese, but they are not the same. *Shibaraku* means "for a while," as in

1. しばらくここでお待ち下さい。

   Shibaraku koko de omachi kudasai.

   Please wait here for a while.

   Just as in the case of English "for a while," the time span referred to as *shibaraku* could be either long or not so long; only the context determines the actual length.

   Shibarakuburi, on the other hand, means "for the first time after a long while," and is never used unless the time span is long. It is thus synonymous with *hisashiburi,* as in

2. 今日は しばらくぶり に／で 日本映画を見た。
            久しぶり

   Kyoo wa shibarakuburi ni/de Nihon-eiga o mita.
         hisashiburi

   Today I saw a Japanese film after a long time.

   When you see someone after many months or years, you may exchange the following greeting, which is a standard formula used quite often:

3. （お）久しぶり ですね。
    しばらくぶり

   (O)hisashiburi desu ne.
   Shibarakuburi

   We haven't seen each other for a long time.

   When the person you meet in such a situation is a good friend with whom you speak informally, just say

4. しばらく！

   Shibaraku!

   Haven't seen you for a while!

In this case, *-buri* is omitted. Note that *-buri* in *hisashi-buri,* however, can never be left out, i.e., "hisashi" by itself can never be used.

SHIGOTO 仕事 work, job

Shigoto means "job" or "work."

1.(a) ジョンは大学を卒業してすぐ仕事が見つかった。
Jon wa daigaku o sotsugyoo-shite sugu shigoto ga mitsukatta.
John found a job right after he graduated from college.

(b) 今日は会社で仕事がなくて退屈してしまった。
Kyoo wa kaisha de shigoto ga nakute taikutsu-shite shimatta.
Today I was bored at the office because there was no work to do.

In English, one may say "I just came home from work" to mean "I just came home from the office." In Japanese, however, *shigoto* cannot replace *kaisha* "company; office."

2. 今会社（＊仕事）から帰ってきたところです。
Ima kaisha (*shigoto) kara kaette kita tokoro desu.
I just came home from the office.

An American once said to me *Shigoto kara denwa o kakemasu* to mean "I'll call you from my office." This sentence is also wrong. *Shigoto* in this context must be replaced by *kaisha, ginkoo* "bank," *daigaku, kenkyuujo* "institute," etc., depending on where one works; otherwise just use *tsutomesaki* "place where one is employed."

SHIKATA GA NAI 仕方がない cannot be helped

Shikata ga nai is almost always equated with "cannot be helped," as in

1. 病気の時に学校を休むのは仕方がない。
   Byooki no toki ni gakkoo o yasumu no wa shikata ga nai.
   Missing school when one is ill is something that can't be helped.

   This expression, however, has other uses. For example, it may mean "useless" when preceded by *te mo.*
2. 今さらそんなことを言っても仕方がない。
   Imasara sonna koto o itte mo shikata ga nai.
   It's useless to say that kind of thing now.

   Or it may mean "unbearably" when preceded by te.
3. 暑くて仕方がないから、プールへ行こうと思う。
   Atsukute shikata ga nai kara, puuru e ikoo to omou.
   It's unbearably hot (lit., It's so hot and there's nothing we can do about it); I think I'll go to the pool.

   It also means "hopeless" when it directly modifies a noun.
4. あいつほんとに仕方がないやつだ。
   Aitsu honto ni shikata ga nai yatsu da.
   He's a really hopeless guy.

SHINJIRU 信じる **to believe**

English "believe" is sometimes used very lightly, just to signify "think," as in

1. I believe (or think) I'll have lunch now.

   Shinjiru cannot be used in this manner; it is a much weightier word, as in
2. 私の言うことを信じて下さい。
   Watashi no iu koto o shinjite kudasai.
   Please believe what I say.

   Shinjiru has another version *shinzuru,* but this latter verb is more formal and is basically a written form.
3. キリストを信ずる者はクリスチャンである。
   kirisuto o shinzuru mono wa Kurisuchan de aru.
   A person who believes in Christ is a Christian.

SHINKANSEN 新幹線 **the New Trunk Line; the train which runs on the New Trunk Line**

Shinkansen, the so-called Bullet Train, literally means "New Trunk Line." The word may refer to either the line or the train.

1.(a) 新幹線は６０年代に開通した。
   Shinkansen wa rokujuu-nendai ni kaitsuu-shita.
   The Shinkansen opened in the 60's.

(b) 今度の京都行きの新幹線は何時に出ますか。
   Kondo no Kyooto-yuki no Shinkansen wa nan-ji ni demasu ka.
   What time is the next Shinkansen leaving for Kyoto?

   This kind of ambiguous usage is quite common in Japanese and is seen widely. English tends to be a little more specific. Compare the Japanese and the English versions below.

2.   今度の日航は九時に出ます。
   Kondo no Nikkoo wa ku-ji ni demasu.
   The next Japan Airlines flight leaves at 9 a.m.

SHINTAISHOOGAISHA 身体障害者 **physically-handicapped person**

Just as English has become very sensitive about the use of discriminatory expressions such as "blind," "deaf," "mute," "cripple," etc., so has Japanese. Although the Japanese public in general still remains insensitive, the media have become extremely careful not to use any discriminatory terms. In fact, more and more neutral-sounding new words are being coined for this purpose. For example, a deaf person used to be called *tsunbo,* but the official term these days is *roosha* 聾者, which sounds much less offensive. *Shintaishoogaisha* is another fairly new word meaning "physically-handicapped person." Since it is such a long word consisting of five kanji, it is often shortened to *shinshoosha* 身障者, using only the first, third, and last kanji.

SHIRITSU 私立 private

In a Japanese-English dictionary, *shiritsu* 私立 is always translated as "private," but this is actually very misleading because the idea of "private" is expressed only by the first kanji of the two, and not by the second, which is 立, meaning "established" or "founded." A private university is a privately-established university, so it is *shiritsu-daigaku* 私立大学. A private property, however, is a privately-owned, not privately established, property, so you must call it *shiyuu-zaisan* 私有財産 (lit., "privately-owned property"), not *shiritsu-zaisan.* A private hospital room is called *koshitsu* 個室 (lit., "individual room").

Shiritsu-daigaku 私立大学 "private university" and *shiritsu-daigaku* 市立大学 "municipal university" (lit., city-founded university) are unfortunately pronounced the same. To make the distinction clear in speech, the former is often pronounced *watakushi-ritsu,* giving a *kun* reading to the first kanji 私, which is normally given an *on* reading in this context. 市 *shi* in 市立大学, too, is pronounced sometimes with its *kun* reading, i.e., *ichi,* for the sake of differentiation.

SHISOO 思想 thought; idea; ideology

English "thought" and "idea" are words that can be used in daily speech, e.g., "I'll give it a thought," "That's a good idea," etc. *Shisoo,* on the other hand, is a more technical, academic, philosophical term, as in

1.(a) カントの思想

   Kanto no shisoo

   Kant's ideology

   (b) 近代思想史

   kindaishisooshi

   modern intellectual history

For "I'll give it a thought," therefore, just say *Chotto kangaete mimasu.* For "That's a good idea," say *Ii kangae da,* or even *Ii aidia da,* but not **Ii shisoo da.*

SHOKUJI 食事 meal

In English, you can say either "have a meal" or "eat a meal." In Japanese, however, use *shokuji o suru* (lit., "do a meal") or, more formally, *shokuji o toru* (lit., "take a meal"), but not **shokuji o taberu.*

Gohan 御飯, when used in the sense of "meal," on the other hand, takes *taberu,* and not *suru* or *toru.* See the example below.

1. 御飯もう食べた（＊した／取った）？

   Gohan moo tabeta (*shita/totta)?

   Have you eaten yet? (lit., Have you eaten a meal yet?)

SHUMI 趣味 hobby; taste

Shumi has two meanings. First, it is something one does for fun in one's spare time, as in

1. 私の趣味は読書とスポーツです。

   Watashi no shumi wa dokusho to supootsu desu.

   My hobbies are reading and sports.

Second, *shumi* means "ability to see and enjoy what is good in art, manners, etc.," as in

2.　吉田さんの着ているものは、いつも趣味がいい。

Yoshida-san no kite-iru mono wa, itsumo shumi ga ii.

Ms. Yoshida's clothes always show good taste.

SHUSHOO 首相 prime minister

In English, "prime minister" and "premier" may refer to the same person. In Japanese, there are *shushoo* and *sooridaijin,* but the former is used more frequently than the latter. *Sooridaijin* is often shortened to just *soori.*

1.　きょう首相／総理(大臣)はイギリスの首相と会談の予
　　定だそうだ。

Kyoo shushoo/soori(daijin) wa Igirisu no shushoo to kaidan no yotei da soo da.

I hear the premier is scheduled to have a meeting with the prime minister of England today.

Interestingly, *soori(daijin)* is rarely used in reference to the prime minister of a foreign nation.

SHUJUTSU 手術 (surgical) operation

Shujutsu refers to "surgical operation," and not any other kind of operation. "Be operated on" is formally *shujutsu o ukeru* (lit., "receive an operation").

1.　佐藤さんは来月胃の手術を受けることになっている。

Satoo-san wa raigetsu i no shujutsu o ukeru koto ni natte iru.

Mr. Sato is scheduled to have a stomach operation next month.

"To operate on someone" is *shujutsu o suru,* as in

2.　外科医は手術をするのが専門だ。

Gekai wa shujutsu o suru no ga senmon da.

Surgeons specialize in operating.

Colloquially, however, *shujutsu o suru* is often used to mean the same as *shujutsu o ukeru.*

3.　佐藤さんは来月胃の手術をするんだって。

Satoo-san wa raigetsu i no shujutsu o suru n datte.

I hear Mr. Sato is going to have a stomach operation next month.

In informal speech, *shujutsu* is frequently pronounced *shujitsu* just as *Shinjuku* is often pronounced *Shinjiku.*

SHUUSEN 終戦 end of the war

August 15 is commemorated in Japan as *Shuusen Kinenbi* "the day to commemorate the end of World War II." What is interesting is the fact that the Japanese rarely use the word *haisen* "defeat (in war)" because it hurts their egos too much to admit the war ended in Japan's surrender. Hence *shuusen,* which they can swallow more easily. Although some people criticize this hypocrisy, it may not be a bad practice. After all, *shuusen* is not a lie. The war did end that day.

SUGOI すごい terrific

Sugoi used to be nothing more than an adjective, as in

1.(a)　あの女性はすごい美人だ。

Ano josei wa sugoi bijin da.

That woman is a striking beauty.

(b)　すごい雨だね。

Sugoi ame da ne.

Isn't this an awful downpour!

Nowadays, in colloquial Japanese, it is sometimes used as an adverb as well, as in 2.

2. このケーキすごいおいしいね。

   Kono keeki sugoi oishii ne.

   Doesn't this cake taste great?

In traditional speech, *sugoku oishii* used to be the norm. Even today, *sugoi* as an adverb is still substandard, but it is becoming quite common among young people speaking casually.

SUKI 好き to like

American students of Japanese often misuse the word *suki*. The worst example might be the following:

1. A：ロマンチックな映画が好きですか。

   Romanchikku na eiga ga suki desu ka.

   Do you like romantic movies?

   B：＊ええ、ときどき好きです。

   *Ee, tokidoki suki desu.

   Yes, I do like them sometimes.

In English, it is certainly all right to say "I like them sometimes," but in Japanese, *suki* cannot be used like this because the word may be used only in reference to a sustained state, and not to an occasional occurrence. The answer above should be:

2. ええ、好きですよ。ときどきいいのがありますから。

   Ee, suki desu yo. Tokidoki ii no ga arimasu kara.

   Yes, I do. Sometimes there are good ones.

   (See also SUKI in *JWTU1*.)

SUMIMASEN 済みません I'm sorry; thank you.

Sumimasen is basically a form of apology. If a student is scolded by his/her teacher, the best thing to do is to bow, saying *Sumimasen* ("I'm sorry").

Sumimasen is increasingly used as an expression of thanks, too. If someone gives you a gift, you accept it with a bow, saying *Doomo sumimasen* ("Thank you very much"). Although purists are against this use—saying that a word of apology should not be used to express gratitude—it is so common nowadays that no one can stem the tide. The reason this has happened is because in the minds of Japanese people, apologizing and thanking are very similar. The Japanese apologize when they have done something wrong and feel they have to repay for that; they express gratitude when someone does something for them for which they feel they have to repay. Both involve the feeling of owing something to someone.

Incidentally, in English, it is perfectly in accordance with decorum to say "Pardon me?" or "I beg your pardon?" when one fails to catch what someone has just said. However, do not translate this into **Sumimasen?* when you are speaking Japanese. The most common expression in that case would be *Ha?* in formal speech, and *E?* in informal speech. In other words, if you want a higher-status person to repeat, say *Ha?*, and if you want a friend to repeat, say *E?* Even though this *Ha?* unfortunately sounds somewhat like English "Huh?", it is a polite expression which is totally acceptable. You must not feel shy about using it.

SUMOO 相撲 sumo wrestling; sumo wrestler

Sumoo means both "sumo wrestling," as in 1, and "professional sumo wrestler," as in 2.

1. 相撲は、するスポーツと言うより、見るスポーツだ。
   Sumoo wa, suru supootsu to iu yori, miru supootsu da.
   Sumo is a spectator sport rather than a participatory sport.

2. 千代の富士はりっぱな相撲だった。

Chiyonofuji wa rippa na sumoo datta.

Chiyonofuji was a great sumo wrestler.

In the second sense, *sumoo* may be replaced by *sumootori* (lit., "person who does sumo"), *rikishi,* or *osumoosan.* Of these three, the last one is the most colloquial version.

SUWARU 座る **to sit down**

"Sitting down" in general is *suwaru* whether one sits on a floor or in a chair. There is another verb *(koshi)kakeru,* which means "sit down (in a chair, on a bench, sofa, etc.)" but not "sit down on a floor." In the following examples, therefore, *koshikaketa* is correct in 1(a), but not in 1(b).

1.(a) ソファーに座った (or 腰かけた)。

Sofaa ni suwatta (or **koshikaketa**).

I sat down on the sofa.

(b) たたみに座った (not 腰掛けた)。

Tatami ni suwatta (* **koshikaketa**).

I sat down on the tatami.

Suwaru is a verb expressing the momentary action of sitting down. *Suwatte-iru,* therefore does not mean "someone is in the process of sitting down," but rather "someone is in the state of having sat down," i.e., someone is in a sitting position. *Koshikakeru* also is a momentary verb and is used likewise.

2. あそこに座っている (or 腰かけている)人は、大山さんじゃないでしょうか。

Asoko ni suwatte-iru (or **koshikakete-iru**) **hito wa Ooyama-san ja nai deshoo ka.**

Isn't that Ms. Oyama sitting over there?

(See also KAKERU.)

TABEMONO 食べ物 food

The difference between *tabemono* and "food" is that *tabemono* implies "prepared food" while the English equivalent does not. For example, uncooked rice is "food," but not *tabemono*. In English, you go to the supermarket to buy groceries or food. In Japanese, on the other hand, you go to the supermarket to buy *shokuryoohin* "groceries," not t*abemono*.

1.　A：どんな食べ物が好きですか。

　　Donna tabemono ga suki desu ka.
　　What kind of food do you like?

　　B：やっぱりすしですね。

　　Yappari sushi desu ne.
　　Sushi (as might be expected).

2.　日本人は毎日のように食料品（＊食べ物）を買いに行く。

　　Nihonjin wa mainichi no yoo ni shokuryoohin (*tabemono) o kai ni iku.
　　Japanese people go grocery shopping almost every day.

TABITABI たびたび, 度々 often, frequently

Tabitabi is synonymous with such words as *yoku* and *shibashiba*.

1.　日本ではたびたび（よく、しばしば）地震がある。

　　Nihon de wa tabitabi (yoku, shibashiba) jishin ga aru.
　　They often have earthquakes in Japan.

　　Of these three, *yoku* is the most commonly used, *tabitabi* comes in second, and *shibashiba* is definitely reserved for writing. *Tabitabi* and *shibashiba* are nothing more than frequency words, but *yoku* can mean other things such as "well" (See YOKU in *JWTU1*). The following sentence is correct with any of the three words, but *yoku* may imply more than *tabitabi* and *shibashiba*.

2. 日本海沿岸はたびたび（しばしば、よく）雪が降る。

Nihonkai-engan wa tabitabi (shibashiba, yoku) yuki ga furu.

Along the Japan Sea, it often snows.

While *tabitabi* and *shibashiba* simply refer to the frequency of the snowfalls, *yoku yuki ga furu* may imply "it snows a lot" as well as "it often snows."

TAIKEN 体験 experience

Keiken is the most frequently used word for "experience," as in

1.(a) あの会社は、経験の十分な人しか雇わないそうだ。

Ano kaisha wa, keiken no juubun na hito shika yato-wanai soo da.

That company hires only people with sufficient experience, I hear.

(b) 外国人に日本語を教えた経験がありますか。

Gaikokujin ni Nihongo o oshieta keiken ga arimasu ka.

Have you had any experience in teaching Japanese to foreigners?

Taiken also means "experience," but it emphasizes the fact that something was experienced "with one's own body," i.e., first-hand.

2. 戦争を体験してみると、戦争のこわさが分かるようになる。

Sensoo o taiken-shite miru to, sensoo no kowasa ga wakaru yoo ni naru.

By experiencing war first-hand, one begins to understand its horrors.

Keiken could be used in 2, too, but then the sentence would just mean "by living through war," whereas *taiken* would bring up more vivid images of bombings and other horrors.

TAISETSU 大切 important

Taisetsu is quite similar to *daiji*.

1. 一番大切 (or 大事)な人は自分の母親だと思っている人は多いだろう。

   Ichiban taisetsu (or daiji) na hito wa jibun no hahaoya da to omotte-iru hito wa ooi daroo.

   I'm sure there are lots of people who think their mother is the most important person.

As the above example indicates, *taisetsu* (or *daiji*) is subjective, i.e., important to a particular person. In other words, if someone is *taisetsu* to you, you consider him/her dear to your heart. *Taisetsu* (or *daiji*) *na mono* is something you cherish.

Juuyoo also means "important," but it is objective rather than subjective, and signifies "important in terms of a specific role," as in

2. 三島由紀夫は、昭和文学史上重要（＊大切／大事）な作家であった。

   Mishima Yukio wa, Shoowabungakushi-joo juuyoo (*taisetsu/daiji) na sakka de atta.

   Yukio Mishima was an important writer in terms of the literary history of the Showa Period.

Since Sentence 2 concerns Mishima's importance in terms of his role in the literary history of Showa, *juuyoo* is more appropriate than *taisetsu/daiji*.

Taisetsu and *daiji* are often used with *ni suru*, but *juuyoo* is never used that way, e.g.

3. 人間は体を大切／大事（＊重要）にしなければいけない。

   Ningen wa karada o taisetsu/daiji (*juuyoo) ni shinakereba ikenai.

   One must take care of oneself (lit., one's body).

TANOMU 頼む **to request; ask (a favor)**

English "ask" has two basic meanings: "request," as in "I asked him to help me," or "inquire," as in "I asked him about his job." Japanese *tanomu,* on the other hand, may be used for "request," but not for "inquire."

1. 私は、助けてくれるようにと彼に頼んだ。
    Watashi wa, tasukete kureru yoo ni to kare ni tanonda.
    I asked him to help me.
2. 私は彼の仕事についてきいた(＊頼んだ)。
    Watashi wa, kare no shigoto ni tsuite kiita (*tanonda).
    I asked him a question about his job.

TAORERU 倒れる **to fall (over); collapse**

Taoreru may be used for either animate beings that are standing or inanimate objects, as in

1.(a) 電車の中で、前に立っていた人が急に倒れたのでびっくりした。
    Densha no naka de, mae ni tatte-ita hito ga kyuu ni taoreta node bikkuri-shita.
    I was surprised on the train when someone standing in front of me suddenly collapsed.

  (b) 台風で木が何本も倒れた。
    Taifuu de ki ga nan-bon mo taoreta.
    A lot of trees fell because of the typhoon.

Korobu is also translated as "fall," but it is used only for animate beings that are in motion, e.g., walking, running, etc.

2. 雪の日は、すべって転ぶ(＊倒れる)人が多い。
    Yuki no hi wa, subette korobu (*taoreru) hito ga ooi.
    On a snowy day, lots of people slip and fall.

  In Sentence 2, *taoreru,* which refers to the falling of someone who is standing, cannot be used.

TASHIKA たしか、確か **certain; if I remember correctly**

When *tashika* is used as a *na*-adjective, it means "sure, certain, definite."

1.(a) それは確かなことだ。

    Sore wa tashika na koto da.

    That's a sure thing.

  (b) 東京の夏が蒸し暑いのは確かだ。

    Tookyoo no natsu ga mushiatsui no wa tashika da.

    It is certain that summer in Tokyo is muggy.

    When *tashika* is used as an adverb, the meaning changes to "if I remember correctly."

2.   A: 東京の人口はどのぐらいですか。

    Tookyoo no jinkoo wa dono gurai desu ka.

    What's the population of Tokyo?

    B: たしか一千万ぐらいだと思いますが。

    Tashika issenman gurai da to omoimasu ga.

    If I remember correctly, it's about 10,100,000.

Don't confuse this adverbial use with *tashika ni* "certainly."

3.   東京はたしかに大都市だ。

    Tookyoo wa tashika ni daitoshi da.

    Tokyo is certainly a big city.

TASSHA 達者 **healthy; skillful**

Tassha has two meanings. First, it means "healthy," as in

1.   ご両親はお達者ですか。

    Goryooshin wa otassha desu ka.

    Are your parents well?

    In this sense, it may be replaced by *(o)genki.*

    Second, *tassha* means "skillful."

2.   小林さんは英語が達者だ。
   Kobayashi-san wa Eigo ga tassha da.
   Mr. Kobayashi is good at English.
   In this sense, *tassha* is synonymous with *joozu.*

TASUKARU 助かる to be saved, relieved, etc.

Tasukaru is the intransitive counterpart of *tasukeru* "to help/ to save (someone)," and is used mainly in reference to animate beings. There is no close one-word English equivalent.

1.(a)   先生があしたの試験をやめてくれると助かるんだけれど。
   Sensei ga ashita no shiken o yamete kureru to tasukaru n da keredo.
   I wish our teacher would cancel tomorrow's exam. (Implication: We would be greatly relieved then.)

 (b)   兄が宿題を手伝ってくれて本当に助かった。
   Ani ga shukudai o tetsudatte kurete hontoo ni tasukatta.
   My brother helped me with my homework. That was a great help.

   When something happens that gives us great relief, we mumble to ourselves:

2.   ああ、助かった！
   Aa, tasukatta!
   Thank Heaven!

TATAKAU 戦う to fight; wage war; do battle

Tatakau is a written expression and is not used in normal conversation. It is used for real battles or wars.

1.   日本は第二次大戦でアメリカを敵として戦った。
   Nihon wa Dainijitaisen de Amerika o teki to shite tatakatta.
   In World War II, Japan fought with the U.S. as its enemy.

Sentence 2 below sounds strange because *tatakau* is not used in the sense of "to quarrel" or "to have a fist fight."

2.　＊私は大きな人とは戦わないことにしています。

*Watashi wa ooki na hito to wa tatakawanai koto ni shite-imasu.

It's my policy not to fight big guys.

In this sense, use *kenka o suru* "to have a fight" instead.

3.　私は大きな人とはけんかをしないことにしています。

Watashi wa ooki na hito to wa kenka o shinai koto ni shite-imasu.

It's my policy not to fight big guys.

TATERU 建てる **to build**

English "build" may be used for all kinds of things: one may build a bridge, house, road, ship, dam, etc. All of these require different verbs in Japanese unless one uses *tsukuru* "make." *Tateru* "build," however, has a limited use. You can say *ie/biru/apaato o tateru* "build a house/building/apartment house," but for other things such as *hashi* "bridge," *dooro* "road," *fune* "ship," and *damu* "dam," you need other verbs such as *kensetsu-suru* and *kenzoo-suru*.

1.　橋／道路／ダムを建設する／つくる

hashi/dooro/damu o kensetsu-suru

build/make a bridge/road/dam

2.　船を建造する／つくる

fune o kenzoo-suru/tsukuru

build/make a ship

TAZUNERU 訪ねる、尋ねる to visit; inquire

Tazuneru is written in two different kanji, depending on the meaning. First, if it's written 訪ねる, it means "to visit someone or some place."

1.(a) 大阪へ行った時、山田さんを訪ねた。

 Oosaka e itta toki, Yamada-san o tazuneta.

 When I went to Osaka, I visited Mr. Yamada.

 (b) 私は去年 50 年ぶりで奈良を訪ねた。

 Watashi wa kyonen 50-nen-buri de Nara o tazuneta.

 Last year I visited Nara for the first time in fifty years.

訪ねる is a formal expression. The above sentences would become more colloquial if changed as follows:

2.(a) 大阪へ行った時、山田さんに会いに行った。

 Oosaka e itta toki, Yamada-san ni ai ni itta.

 When I went to Osaka, I went to see Mr. Yamada.

 (b) 私は去年 50 年ぶりで奈良へ行った。

 Watashi wa kyonen 50-nen-buri de Nara e itta.

 Last year I went to Nara for the first time in fifty years.

Second, if written 尋ねる, *tazuneru* means "to inquire," as in

3. 田中さんに尋ねたいことがあって、電話をかけた。

 Tanaka-san ni tazune-tai koto ga atte, denwa o kaketa.

 I called Mr. Tanaka to inquire about something.

尋ねる is also a formal expression. In normal conversation, *kiku* is used far more often, as in

4. 田中さんにききたいことがあって、電話をかけた。

 Tanaka-san ni kiki-tai koto ga atte, denwa o kaketa.

 I called Mr. Tanaka to ask about something.

TENKI 天気 weather

Don't confuse *tenki* "weather" with *kikoo* "climate." *Tenki* is short range while *kikoo* is long range. Therefore, *tenki* is correct in 1(a), but not in 1(b).

1.(a) 今日の天気（＊気候）は晴れのち曇りだそうだ。

Kyoo no tenki (*kikoo) wa hare nochi kumori da soo da.

They say today's weather will be sunny first, and cloudy later.

(b) カリフォルニアの気候（＊天気）は一年中温暖だ。

Kariforunia no kikoo (*tenki) wa ichi-nen-juu ondan da.

California's climate is mild throughout the year.

American students of Japanese often make the following errors:

2.(a) ＊今日は暑い (or 寒い） 天気ですねえ！

*Kyoo wa atsui (or samui) tenki desu nee!

Don't we have pretty hot/cold weather today?

(b) ＊今日は天気が暑い (or 寒い） ですねえ！

*Kyoo wa tenki ga atsui (or samui) desu nee!

Isn't the weather pretty hot/cold today?

Unlike Enlish "weather," Japanese *tenki* basically goes with adjectives like *ii* "good" and *iya na* "nasty," and not normally with *atsui* or *samui.* Instead of 2(a)/2(b) above, say:

3. 今日は暑い(or 寒い)ですねえ！

Kyoo wa atsui (or samui) desu nee!

Isn't it pretty hot/cold today?

TO ISSHO NI と一緒に **together with**

American students who have returned to the U.S. after a year's study in Japan often talk about their homestay experience as follows:

1. ？日本人のホストファミリーと一緒に住んでいました。

? Nihonjin no hosutofamirii to issho ni sunde-imashita.

I was living with a Japanese host family.

This sentence, however, sounds very strange in Japanese. Basically *to issho ni* is used when the two parties involved are on an equal footing. In Sentence 2, for example, *to issho ni* is correctly used.

2. 日本人の友達と一緒に住んでいました。

   Nihonjin no tomodachi to issho ni sunde-imashita.

   I was living with a Japanese friend.

   When you do a homestay, however, you are a renter/boarder while the host family is the owner of the house. Sentences 3(a) and 3(b) therefore sound much more natural than Sentence 1.

3.(a) 日本人のホストファミリーの家 (or 所) に住んでいました。

   Nihonjin no hosutofamirii no ie (or tokoro) ni sunde-imashita.

   I was living at the home of a Japanese host family.

  (b) 日本人の家でホームステイをしました。

   Nihonjin no ie de hoomusutei o shimashita.

   I did a homestay at a Japanese home.

TOJIRU 閉じる to close (something)

For some objects, *shimeru* cannot be used to mean "to close (something)." *Tojiru* must be used instead. Three good examples of those objects are *hon* "book," *me* "eye," and *kuchi* "mouth."

1. 本を閉じて (＊しめて) 下さい。

   Hon o tojite (*shimete) kudasai.

   Please close your book.

2. 座禅の時は、目を閉じる (＊しめる) ことになっている。

   Zazen no toki wa, me o tojiru (*shimeru) koto ni natte-iru.

   When you do zazen, you are expected to close your eyes.

3. うるさいね。口を閉じなさい (＊しめなさい)。

   Urusai ne. Kuchi o tojinasai (*shimenasai).

   You talk too much. Close your mouth.

TOKAI 都会 **(big) city**

Tokai means "city," especially "big city," as in
1.　私はいなかより都会に住み慣れている。
　　Watashi wa inaka yori tokai ni sumi-narete-iru.
　　I am more used to living in a big city than in a rural area.
　　Toshi also means "(big) city" but, in speech, it is rarely used by itself. Rather it is more often used as part of a compound, as in
2.(a)　工業都市（＊都会）
　　koogyootoshi (*tokai)
　　industrial city
　(b)　都市（＊都会）計画
　　toshi (*tokai) keikaku
　　city planning

TOKORODE ところで **by the way; incidentally**

Tokorode is used when you change a conversational topic completely. Suppose you have been talking about something and suddenly want to talk about a new topic. *Tokorode* would be the right word to use.
1.　(A and B talk about professional baseball first, but then A feels like talking about something else.)
　　A: ジャイアンツ負けましたね。
　　Jaiants makemashita ne.
　　The Giants lost, didn't they?
　　B: そうですね。このごろよく負けますね。
　　Soo desu ne. Konogoro yoku makemasu ne.
　　Yes, they did. They have been losing a lot of games lately.

A: ところで、Bさん。このごろゴルフの方はどうですか。

Tokorode, B-san. Konogoro gorufu no hoo wa doo desuka.

On another note, Mr. B., how's your golf game these days?

Sate, too, is used to change topics and may be translated as "by the way" or "incidentally," but there are at least two differences between *sate* and *tokorode*. First, *sate* is often used without a preceding conversation, i.e., just to indicate switching to a new action. Suppose you have been watching TV and suddenly decide to take a walk. You may mumble to yourself or someone around you,

2. さて（＊ところで）散歩に出かけようか。

Sate (*Tokorode) sanpo ni dekakeyoo ka.

Well, I guess I'll go for a walk now.

Second, *sate* indicates the conversation that is to follow is more important than the preceding one. For example, suppose you go to visit someone to talk business. At first, you just exchange small talk for a few minutes, talking about the weather or some timely events. You then wish to indicate the true intention of your visit.

3. さて今日伺ったわけは・・・

Sate kyoo ukagatta wake wa . . .

By the way, the reason I came to see you today was . . .

In this case, *tokorode* could be used, too, but it would just indicate you are switching to a new topic, whereas *sate* signals the fact that the new topic will be more important.

TOOJI 当時 **in those days**

Tooji, which means "in those days," refers to a period of time in the past—not in the recent past, but rather a number of years ago.

1. 私は十二歳の時初恋をした。当時私は中学の一年生だった。

   Watashi wa juuni-sai no toki hatsukoi o shita. Tooji watashi wa chuugaku no ichi-nensei datta.

   I experienced my first love when I was twelve. In those days, I was a seventh grader.

   Since *tooji* refers to a period of time, but not a point of time, it cannot be used in the following sentence.

2. 高校時代のある日、私は銀座へ買い物に行ったのだが、その時(＊当時)意外な人に会った。

   Kookoo-jidai no aru hi, watashi wa Ginza e kaimono ni itta no da ga, sono toki (*tooji) igai na hito ni atta.

   One day when I was in high school, I went shopping in the Ginza; I bumped into an unexpected person then.

   Tooji is replaceable by *sono koro,* but is more formal than the latter.

TOONAN 東南 **southeast**

In English, "southeast" can refer to either a location (e.g., Southeast Asia) or a direction (e.g., "if you drive southeast, you'll come to a big river"). In Japanese, for location, *toonan* (lit., "eastsouth") is the norm, as in

1. 東南アジア

   Toonan Ajia

   Southeast Asia (lit., Eastsouth Asia)

   For direction, follow the same pattern as English.

2. 南東の風

   Nantoo no kaze

   southeasterly wind

TOOZAINANBOKU 東西南北 lit., east-west-south-north

In English, the four directions are usually referred to as "north-south-east-west," in that order. In Japanese, however, they follow a different order 東西南北, lit. "east-west-south-north." This particular order was originally introduced from China.

TORI 鳥 bird; chicken

Tori, first of all, means "bird."

1. 日本にいる鳥の種類は減ってきている。
   Nihon ni iru tori no shurui wa hette-kite-iru.
   The number of bird species in Japan is decreasing.

   Second, *tori is* used as an abbreviation of *toriniku,* which means "chicken" (lit., "bird meat").

2. 牛が高いので、このごろは鳥ばかり食べている。
   Gyuu ga takai node, konogoro wa tori bakari tabete-iru.
   Since beef is expensive, we've been eating nothing but chicken these days.

TSUIDE NI ついでに taking the opportunity while doing something else

Tsuide ni is used when one takes the opportunity to do something while doing something else.

1. 散歩に行ったついでに、スーパーに寄って買い物をした。
   Sanpo ni itta tsuide ni, suupaa ni yotte kaimono o shita.
   I stopped by the supermarket for some shopping while I was out taking a walk.

2.　Husband:　ちょっとタバコを買ってくるよ。

Chotto tabako o katte kuru yo.

I'm going out to buy cigarettes.

　　　Wife:　じゃ、ついでにこれポストに入れてきて。

Ja, tsuide ni kore posuto ni irete kite.

Will you mail this then? (lit., Will you take that opportunity to mail this?)

Don't forget the fact that both actions must be volitional (i.e., intentionally done). Sentences 3(a) and 3(b) are wrong because, in each of them, one of the events described is involuntary.

3.(a)　＊天気がよくなったついでに洗濯をした。

*Tenki ga yoku natta tsuide ni sentaku o shita.

When the weather improved, taking that opportunity, I did the wash.

(b)　＊散歩に行ったついでに、思いがけない人に出会った。

*Sanpo ni itta tsuide ni, omoigakenai hito ni deatta.

When I went out for a walk, I took the opportunity to bump into an unexpected person.

Since, in 3(a), *tenki ga yokunatta* "the weather improved" is not a controllable action, *tsuide ni* may not be used. The sentence must be restated as follows:

4.　天気がよくなったので、洗濯をした。

Tenki ga yoku natta node, sentaku o shita.

Since the weather improved, I did the wash.

In Sentence 3(b), *tsuide ni* is inappropriate because bumping into someone is an involuntary event. The sentence must be restated as follows:

5.　散歩の途中で思いがけない人に出会った。

Sanpo no tochuu de omoigakenai hito ni deatta.

While taking a walk, I bumped into an unexpected person.

TSUKARERU 疲れる   **to become tired**

Americans often forget the fact that *tsukareru* by itself means "to become tired," not just "tired." To mean "I became tired," all one has to say is *Tsukareta* or *Tsukaremashita.* Try not to create the false equivalent of English "I became tired."

1.   あまりテニスをしたので　疲れました。
                                   ＊疲れてになりました。
                                   ＊疲れているになりました。
  Amari tenisu o shita node tsukaremashita.
                                 *tsukarete ni narimashita.
                                 *tsukarete-iru ni narimashita.
   I played so much tennis that I became tired.
   (See also NINSHIN-SURU.)

TSURAI つらい **hard to bear**

Tsurai is often quite similar to *kurushii* "painful." For example, a tough, demanding job can be described as either *tsurai shigoto* or *kurushii shigoto.* However, while *kurushii* focuses more on physical difficulty, *tsurai* is more mental and psychological. Study the following exampless:

1.   子供に死なれるのは　　　　つらい。
                                   ＊苦しい。
  Kodomo ni shinareru no wa tsurai.
                                 *kurushii.
   It's hard to lose a child.
2.   かぜを引いて胸が　　　　　苦しい。
                                   ＊つらい。
  Kaze o hiite mune ga   kurushii.
                                 *tsurai.
   I have a cold, and my chest hurts.

TSURETE-IKU 連れていく **to take (someone) along**

In English, one can say both "take someone along" and "take something along." Whether what one takes along is animate or inanimate makes no difference. In Japanese, however, one must use *tsurete-iku* when the object is a person or an animal, but *motte-iku* when it is inanimate.

1. 子供を映画へ連れていく約束をした。
   Kodomo o eiga e tsurete-iku yakusoku o shita.
   I promised to take my child to a movie.
2. 子供たちは毎日学校へお弁当を持っていく。
   Kodomo-tachi wa mainichi gakkoo e obentoo o motte-iku.
   My children take box lunches to school every day.

Making a distinction between animate beings and inanimate objects is one of the characteristics of the Japanese language, the most basic example being *iru* for animate beings versus *aru* for inanimate objects.

TSUTOMERU 勤める、務める、努める **to become employed; serve as; make efforts**

Tsutomeru has three main meanings, depending on the kanji used. The first one is 勤める, meaning "to become employed," and it usually appears in the -*te* form.

1. 高田さんは銀行に勤めている。
   Takada-san wa ginkoo ni tsutomete-iru.
   Mr. Takada works for a bank. (lit., Mr. Takada is employed at a bank.)

Tsutomeru when written 務める means "to serve as," as in

2. 吉田茂は、何年にもわたって首相を務めた。
   Yoshida Shigeru wa, nan-nen ni mo watatte shushoo o tsutometa.
   Shigeru Yoshida served as Premier for many years.

Tsutomeru when written 努める means "make efforts."

3. 学生は勉学に努めるべきだ。

   Gakusei wa bengaku ni tsutomeru beki da.

   Students should put all their effort into study.

   The second and the third uses above, i.e., 務める and 努める, are fairly formal and are not as common as the first, i.e., 勤める. Sentences 2 and 3 would perhaps be more commonly restated as 4 and 5, respectively.

4. 吉田茂は何年も首相だった。

   Yoshida Shigeru wa nan-nen mo shushoo datta.

   Shigeru Yoshida was Premier for many years.

5. 学生は一生懸命勉強すべきだ。

   Gakusei wa isshookenmei benkyoo-su-beki da.

   Students should study hard.

   (See also TSUTOMERU in *JWTU1*.)

TSUUYAKU 通訳 the art of interpretation; interpreter

Tsuuyaku has two meanings. First, the act of orally translating from one language to another.

1. スミスさんは日本語が出来ないから、日本へ行ったら誰か正しい通訳をしてくれる人が必要だろう。

   Sumisu-san wa Nihongo ga dekinai kara, Nihon e ittara dare ka tadashii tsuuyaku o shite kureru hito ga hitsuyoo daroo.

   Since Mr. Smith doesn't speak Japanese, he will need someone in Japan who can do accurate interpreting for him.

   Second, *tsuuyaku* means someone whose job is interpreting.

2. 日本には英語の出来る通訳は多いが、ロシア語の出来る通訳は少ない。

   Nihon ni wa Eigo no dekiru tsuuyaku wa ooi ga, Roshiago no dekiru tsuuyaku wa sukunai.

   In Japan, there are a lot of interpreters who can speak English, but very few who can handle Russian.

For this second meaning, one may also use *tsuuyakusha,* but this is a formal expression reserved for written language only.

The situation is quite different with *hon'yaku* 翻訳, which means "translation" only, and not "translator." For the latter, one has to use *hon'yakuka* 翻訳家, which means "professional translator" or *yakusha* "translator (of a particular piece of writing)."

UKAGAU 伺う to inquire; visit

Ukagau, first of all, is the humble counterpart of 訪ねる *tazuneru* "to visit."

1. 先生、あした研究室の方へ伺ってもよろしいでしょうか。
   Sensei, ashita ken'kyuushitsu no hoo e ukagatte mo yoroshii deshoo ka.
   Sensei, may I come and see you in the office tomorrow?

   Second, *ukagau* is the humble counterpart of 尋ねる *tazuneru* "to inquire."

2. 先生、ちょっと伺いたいことがあるんですが。
   Sensei, chotto ukagaitai koto ga aru n desu ga.
   Sensei, I have a question I'd like to ask you.

   Although *ukagau* is a humble form to begin with, its humble form also exists, i.e., *oukagai-suru.* For example, *ukagatte mo* in Sentence 1 above could be rephrased *oukagai-shite mo,* and *ukagaitai* in Sentence 2 could be replaced by *oukagai-shitai,* respectively. However, *oukagai-suru* is a double humble verb and may thus sound overly polite to some people.

UN 運 luck; fortune

"Lucky" is *un ga yoi* (or *ii*), lit., "(my) luck is good"; "unlucky" is *un ga warui,* lit., "(my) luck is bad."

1. あんなすばらしい女性と結婚できたなんて、鈴木さんは
   運がいい。

   Anna subarashii josei to kekkon dekita nante, Suzuki-san wa un ga ii.

   Mr. Suzuki is fortunate to have been able to marry such a wonderful woman.

2. 運が悪いことに、ピクニックの日に雨になってしまった。

   Un ga warui koto ni, pikunikku no hi ni ame ni natte shi-matta.

   Unluckily, it started raining on the day of the picnic.

   There is a synonym for *un*, i.e., *unmei*, which means "destiny, fate." *Unmei* cannot be used in Sentences 1 and 2 above, but conversely in Sentence 3 below *unmei* cannot be replaced by *un*.

3. それが私の運命(*運)だったのかもしれない。

   Sore ga watashi no unmei (*un) datta no ka mo shirenai.

   That was perhaps my fate/destiny.

URAYAMASHII 羨ましい envious; enviable

Urayamashii is "envious/enviable."

1. 私はあなたが羨ましい。

   Watashi wa anata ga urayamashii.

   I am envious of you. (lit., As for me, you are enviable.)

   Urayamashii has a corresponding verb *urayamu* "to envy."

2. 人が大きな家を建てたのを羨んではいけない。

   Hito ga ookina ie o tateta no o urayande wa ikenai.

   You mustn't envy someone having built a big house.

As is the case with adjectives of feelings (See also SABISHII), when the person who is envious is not the speaker, *urayamashii* must be changed to a verb, i.e., *urayamashigaru* "to show signs of being envious," or other words such as *rashii* and *yoo* must be added, as in

3.(a) 田中さんはスミスさんの新しいコンピューターを羨ましがっている。

Tanaka-san wa Sumisu-san no atarashii konpyuutaa o urayamashigatte-iru.

Mr. Tanaka is envious (lit., is showing signs of being envious) of Mr. Smith's new computer.

(b) 田中さんはスミスさんの新しいコンピューターが羨ましいらしい／ようだ。

Tanaka-san wa Sumisu-san no atarashii konpyuutaa ga urayamashii rashii/yoo da.

Mr. Tanaka seems to be envious of Mr. Smith's new computer.

WAKU 沸く to boil

Waku is normally "to come to a boil," as in

1. お湯が沸いたから、お茶を入れましょう。

   Oyu ga waita kara, ocha o iremashoo.

   Water has boiled. Let's have tea.

Note the expression to be used is *oyu ga waku* (lit., "hot water boils") and not **mizu ga waku* (lit., "cold water boils").

Another use of *waku* that could be confusing to English speakers is *furo ga waku,* as in

2. お風呂が沸きましたよ。

   Ofuro ga wakimashita yo.

   The bath water has gotten warm enough.

Note that, in this case, the bath water is not really boiling!

WARAU 笑う to laugh

English has a number of verbs that express different kinds of laugh, such as "giggle," "chuckle," and "guffaw." In Japanese, however, *warau* is the basic verb, and one adds onomatopoetic adverbs to describe different types of laugh.

1.(a) くすくす笑う
   kusukusu warau
   to giggle

 (b) くつくつ笑う
   kutsukutsu warau
   to chuckle

 (c) げらげら笑う
   geragera warau
   to guffaw

   Kinds of smile, too, are expressed in a similar way, i.e., by adding onomatopoetic adverbs.

2.(a) にこっと笑う
   nikotto warau
   to break into a pleasant smile

 (b) にこにこ笑う
   nikoniko warau
   to smile pleasantly and continuously

 (c) にやにや笑う
   niyaniya warau
   to grin

YAHARI/YAPPARI やっぱり **as might be expected**

When one listens to interviews on TV or on the radio, one is struck by the frequency of the occurrence of *yahari* or its more colloquial variant, *yappari*. For example,

1.   A: Bさんはどんな料理がお好きですか。
      B-san wa donna ryoori ga osuki desu ka.
      What kind of cuisine do you like the best?
     B: やっぱり日本料理ですねえ。
      Yappari Nihonryoori desu nee.
      Japanese food (as you might expect).

2.   A: 今度の春場所は誰が優勝するでしょうか。

     Kondo no harubasho wa dare ga yuushoo-suru deshoo ka.

     Who do you think will win the sumo tournament this spring?

  B: やっぱり貴の花じゃないですか。

     Yappari Takanohana ja nai desu ka.

     Takanohana, I guess (like everybody else).

Yahari/yappari basically signifies "What I'm saying is nothing unusual. It's something you might be expecting to hear. I'm no different from others." In other words, *yahari/yappari* is used frequently because it suits the typical Japanese mind, which does not wish to be too individualistic.

YAKU 約 approximately

Yaku is attached to a numeral to indicate an approximate number/amount. It is synonymous with *gurai*. There are, however, some differences between the two. First, *yaku* sounds more formal than *gurai*. Second, *yaku* must precede a numeral while *gurai* follows, as in

1. ニューヨークには、約十年(or 十年ぐらい)住んでいた。

     Nyuuyooku ni wa, yaku juu-nen (or juu-nen gurai) sunde-ita.

     I lived in New York about ten years.

Another difference is that *yaku* is used only with a number whereas *gurai* does not have to, as in

2. むすこは私と同じぐらい(＊約同じ)の身長です。

     Musuko wa watashi to onaji gurai (*yaku onaji) no shinchoo desu.

     My son is about as tall as I am.

YAKYUU 野球 **baseball**

A number of sports that used to be called by non-Western names before and during World War II are now called by Western names. For example,

shuukyuu	蹴球	→	*sakkaa*	"soccer"
haikyuu	排球	→	*bareebooru*	"volleyball"
rookyuu	篭球	→	*basukettobooru*	"basketball"

Yakyuu "baseball" is an exception. It still is rarely called *beesubooru* even though most people understand the term. Baseball terms, on the other hand, are mostly loanwords, e.g., *pitchaa* "pitcher," *kyatchaa* "catcher," *hitto* "hit," and *fauru* "foul."

In English, "baseball" and "a baseball" are different, the former being the name of a sport and the latter referring to the ball used for baseball. In Japanese, on the other hand, *yakyuu* simply means "baseball," and in order to refer to a baseball, one has to say *yakyuu no booru*, lit., "a baseball ball."

YANE 屋根 **roof**

Yane is "roof," as in

1. このごろの日本では、青や赤の屋根が増えてきたような気がする。

   Konogoro no Nihon de wa, ao ya aka no yane ga fuete-kita yoo na ki ga suru.

   It seems to me that lately blue or red roofs have increased in Japan.

To refer to the roofs of Western-style buildings such as department stores and hotels, however, use *okujoo* instead of *yane,* as in

2. 夏になると、屋上 (＊屋根)にビアガーデンを開くデパートがある。

   Natsu ni naru to, okujoo (*yane) ni biagaaden o hiraku depaato ga aru.

   There are some department stores that open "beer gardens" on their roofs in the summer.

YASUMI 休み rest; vacation

In America, "vacation" often indicates "pleasure trip one takes away from work," as in "He is on vacation in Europe." Japanese *yasumi,* on the other hand, does not suggest "trip" by itself. The following is therefore wrong.

1. ＊小学生のころ、よく両親と休みに行ったことを覚えている。

   ***Shoogakusei no koro, yoku ryooshin to yasumi ni itta koto o oboete-iru.**

   The above sentence was once written by a student of mine to mean "I remember often going on vacation with my parents when I was in elementary school." This student should have written as follows:

2. 小学生のころ、休みになるとよく両親と旅行したことを覚えている。

   Shoogakusei no koro, yasumi ni naru to, yoku ryooshin to ryokoo-shita koto o oboete-iru.

   I remember that, in my elementary school days, I often went on a trip with my parents when vacation time came around.

   (See YASUMI, *JWTU1.*)

YASUMU 休む to rest; to be absent; to go to bed

The basic meaning of *yasumu* is "to rest."

1. 疲れたから、ちょっと休んでいるんです。

   Tsukareta kara, chotto yasunde-iru n desu.

   I'm resting because I'm tired.

   Occasionally, *yasumu* means "to go to bed" or "sleep." In this case, *yasumu* is synonymous with *neru*.

2. (mother speaking to a child) もう十一時だから休んだら（or 寝たら）どう。

   Moo juuichi-ji da kara yasundara (or netara) doo.

   It's already 11 o'clock. Why don't you go to bed?

   Yasumu is also used to mean "to be absent," as in

3. 田中さんは、このごろ病気で会社を休むことが多い。

   Tanaka-san wa, konogoro byooki de kaisha o yasumu koto ga ooi.

   These days, Mr. Tanaka is often absent from the office because of illness.

   Be careful not to confuse *kaisha o yasumu* with *kaisha de yasumu*, which would mean "to rest at the office."

YATSU 奴 guy; fellow

Yatsu means "guy" or "fellow" and is considered a coarse, not refined, expression. It is used mainly by men in informal situations.

1. 吉本って変わってる奴だな。

   Yoshimoto te kawatteru yatsu da na.

   Yoshimoto is a strange guy, isn't he?

   Although it is a coarse word, it is not a profanity like English "bastard." However, it does not belong in polite speech just the same.

2. 吉本さんという方は、ちょっと変わっている方（＊奴）ですね。

   Yoshimoto-san to iu kata wa, chotto kawatte-iru kata (*yatsu) desu ne.

   Mr. Yoshimoto is a strange person, isn't he?

Yatsu sometimes means "thing," as in

3. (customer to a salesclerk) もっと 安い奴がほしいんだけど。
   Motto yasui yatsu ga hoshii n da kedo.
   I'd like a cheaper one.

Kono yatsu, sono yatsu, ano yatsu, dono yatsu become *koitsu, soitsu, aitsu, doitsu,* respectively, as in

4. あいつ(=あのやつ)にくらしい奴だ。
   Aitsu (=Ano yatsu) nikurashii yatsu da.
   He's a detestable guy.

YATTA! やった！ "Hurray!"

Yatta! is a frequently used exclamation of joy uttered when something wonderful happens unexpectedly. For example, children might say this when their parents tell them they are taking them on a vacation to Hawaii.

It seems to me that the usage of *Yatta!* has changed over the years. It used to be used only when someone really did something great. For example, when we were at a baseball game and a batter hit a homerun for the team we were cheering for, we probably uttered the exclamation. Nowadays, however, any happy turn of events seems to cause youngsters to yell out *Yatta!*

YOBU 呼ぶ to call

English "call" may be used in the sense of "to visit," as in "I'll call on Mr. Nakada while I'm in Tokyo." Japanese *yobu* has no such usage. Do not use *yobu* in the following sentence.

1. 金曜日はお医者さんが来る (＊呼ぶ) 日だ。
   Kin'yoobi wa oishasan ga kuru (*yobu) hi da.
   Friday is the day when the doctor calls/comes.
   (See also YOBU in *JWTU1*.)

YOKOSU 寄越す to give/send over (to me)

Yokosu means "to give/send over," but the direction of the movement of the object in question must be toward the speaker. Compare 1 and 2 below.

1. 吉田が久しぶりに年賀状を寄越した。
   Yoshida ga hisashiburi ni nengajoo o yokoshita.
   Yoshida sent me a New Year's card for the first time in many years.

2. この間送った（＊寄越した）本着いた？
   Konoaida okutta (*yokoshita) hon tsuita?
   Has the book I sent you the other day arrived?

Yokosu may not be used when the giver/sender is a higher status person.

3. 高橋先生が久しぶりに年賀状を下さった（＊寄越した）。
   Takahashi-sensei ga hisashiburi ni nengajoo o kudasatta (*yokoshita).
   Professor Takahashi sent me a New Year's card for the first time in many years.

YOMU 読む to read

In English, the following dialogue might very well take place the day after a weekend:

1. A: What did you do yesterday?
   B: I read all day.

What B means in this conversation is that he read, most likely, a book or books. In other words, in English, you don't have to express what you read. In Japanese, on the other hand, *yomu* may not be used that way.

2. A: きのうは、どんなことをしたんですか。
   Kinoo wa, donna koto o shita n desu ka.
   B: ＊一日中読みました。
   *Ichinichi-juu yomimashita.

This dialogue, which is the direct translation of 1, sounds very strange because, in Japanese, B would have to be more specific, as follows:

3.　一日中本を読んでいました。

Ichinichi-juu hon o yonde-imashita.

I was reading a book/books all day.

If you don't want to use *hon o,* you can say the following:

4.　一日中読書をしていました。

Ichinichi-juu dokusho o shite-imashita.

I read all day (lit., I was doing reading all day).

This expression *dokusho* is often used when describing hobbies. For example,

5.　A:　Bさんの趣味は？

B-san no shumi wa?

What are your hobbies?

　　B:　テニスと読書です。

Tenisu to dokusho desu.

They are tennis and reading.

Yomu may be used without an object, however, when the object is clear from the context, as in

6.　A:　『風と共に去りぬ』を読んだことありますか。

"Kaze to tomo ni Sarinu" o yonda koto arimasu ka.

Have you ever read *Gone with the Wind?*

　　B:　ええ、二回も読みましたよ。

Ee, ni-kai mo yomimashita yo.

Yes, I've read it twice.

YON 四 four

The standard Japanese pronunciation of the kanji for "four" used to be *shi.* However, *shi* being homonymous with *shi* 死 "death," the Japanese have started avoiding the pronunciation and using *yon,* the Japanese word for "four."

Very few young people nowadays say *juushi* to signify "fourteen," for example. They definitely prefer *juuyon*.

Likewise, the pronunciation of the kanji 七, "seven," which used to be *shichi,* has become unpopular because *shichi* includes the sound *shi.* It has thus changed to *nana,* the traditional Japanese word for "seven." There may be another reason for avoiding *shichi,* i.e., it sounds too similar to *ichi,* which means "one," because some Japanese speakers, particularly residents of the low-lying section of Tokyo, pronounce *shichi* as *hichi,* which makes the word sound even more like *ichi.*

Also 九, the kanji for "nine," is more often read *kyuu* than *ku,* which used to be the standard reading. *Ku* has come to be avoided because it is homonymous with *ku* 苦, which means "suffering."

YOOSU 様子 appearance; state

Yoosu "appearance" may not be used to mean "facial features." Use *kao* instead.

1. インディアンの顔(＊様子)は、ときどき日本人の顔に似ている。

   Indian no kao (*yoosu) wa, tokidoki Nihonjin no kao ni nite-iru.

   Some American Indians share the same facial features with the Japanese.

   Sono Nihonjin no josei wa Amerikajin no yoo na yoosu datta (lit., "That Japanese woman had the appearance of an American"), therefore, does not really mean "That Japanese woman had American facial features," but rather indicates that she was wearing the kind of clothing an American woman would wear, that she behaved like an American, or that she had the aura of an American.

   Yoosu does not have to be visually perceivable. For example,

2. 彼と電話で話したのだが、何だか様子がおかしかった。

   Kare to denwa de hanashita no da ga, nandaka yoosu ga okashikatta.

   I talked with him by phone; somehow he sounded as though something were wrong.

YOU 酔う to get drunk

"To get drunk" is *you* or *yopparau,* the latter indicating a higher degree of intoxication.

1. 僕は酔うことはあるけど、酔っ払うことはないよ。

   Boku wa you koto wa aru keredo, yopparau koto wa nai yo.

   I sometimes get a little drunk, but never heavily drunk.

   The noun form of *yopparau* is *yopparai* "drunkard."

2. 東京の駅には、夜になると、ときどきベンチに寝ている酔っ払いがいる。

   Tookyoo no eki ni wa, yoru ni naru to, tokidoki benchi ni nete-iru yopparai ga iru.

   At Tokyo railroad stations at night, there are sometimes drunken men who are lying down on platform benches.

   You, unlike *yopparau,* may also be used to refer to psychological, not physical, intoxication, as in

3. チームのメンバーは、全員勝利に酔って(＊酔っ払って)いた。

   Chiimu no membaa wa, zen'in shoori ni yotte-(*yopparatte-)ita.

   The members of the team were all intoxicated with victory.

YUUBIN 郵便 mail

To mean "to send out mail," the most commonly used verb is *dasu,* as in

1. (wife to her husband): 散歩のついでに、この手紙を出して ね。

   Sanpo no tsuide ni, kono tegami o dashite ne.

   If you're going out for a walk, please mail this letter for me.

   "To drop a letter into a mailbox" requires another verb, i.e., *ireru,* as in

2. 駅前のポストに手紙を入れた。

   Eki-mae no posuto ni tegami o ireta.

   I dropped a letter into the mailbox outside the station.

   Interestingly, the word *yuubin* is not used for e-mail. E-mail is officially called *denshi-meeru* "electronic mail," but since it is a little too long, most people just call it *meeru.*

3. メールいただきました。

   Meeru itadakimashita.

   I received your e-mail.

YUUJIN 友人 friend

Yuujin means exactly the same as *tomodachi* but is more formal than the latter.

1. 学生時代からの友人(or 友達)というのは、いいものだ。

   Gakusei-jidai kara no yuujin (or tomodachi) to iu no wa, ii mono da.

   Old friends from one's schooldays are great.

   Tomodachi is sometimes preceded by other nouns to form compounds such as *nomitomodachi* "drinking pal(s)" and *asobitomodachi* "playmate(s)." *Yuujin,* on the other hand, is not used that way.

   (See TOMODACHI in *JWTU1.*)

ZASSHI 雑誌 magazine

In English, "magazine" could be added to the name of a specific magazine, as in "I just bought a *Time* magazine." *Zasshi* has no such usage. You may use the second half of *zasshi* as a suffix, however, as in

1. 今週のタイム誌は、今日出るはずだ。
   Konshuu no Taimu-shi wa, kyoo deru hazu da.
   This week's *Time* magazine is supposed to come out today.

This usage is quite formal and normally occurs only in writing. In conversation, just say *Taimu*.

To indicate "weekly/monthly/quarterly magazine," use the suffix -*shi*. These words may be used in speech as well as in writing.

2. 週刊／月刊／季刊誌
   shuukan/gekkan/kikanshi
   weekly/monthly/quarterly magazine

ZEHI ぜひ by all means; at any cost

Zehi has two basic functions. First, it emphasizes requests. In this case, it is normally accompanied by -*te kudasai,* as in

1. あしたのパーティーには、ぜひいらっしゃって下さい。
   Ashita no paatii ni wa, zehi irasshatte kudasai.
   Please by all means come to tomorrow's party.

Second, *zehi* is used to indicate strong wishes or desires. In this case, it is accompanied by such forms as -*tai* and -*(shi) yoo.*

2.(a) ぜひ息子にいい大学に入ってもらいたいものだ。
   Zehi musuko ni ii daigaku ni haitte morai-tai mono da.
   I strongly hope my son gets into a good university.

(b) 今度ぜひ一緒にゴルフをやりましょう。

Kondo zehi issho ni gorufu o yarimashoo.

Let's be sure to play golf together one of these days.

Zehi is not used with negative verbs. Use *zettai ni* "absolutely," instead, as in

3.(a) あしたは絶対に（＊ぜひ）来ないで下さい。

Ashita wa zettai ni (*zehi) konaide kudasai.

Absolutely, please don't come tomorrow.

(b) 絶対に（＊ぜひ）そんな映画は見たくない。

Zettai ni (*zehi) sonna eiga wa mi-takunai.

I would never wish to see a movie like that.

ZENBU 全部 all

Zenbu may be used in reference to both animate beings and inanimate objects, but it probably sounds better when used with inanimate objects.

1. 日本人が全部 (or 日本人全部が／日本人の全部が) 礼儀正しいわけではない。

Nihonjin ga zenbu (or Nihonjin zenbu ga/Nihonjin no zenbu ga) reigitadashii wake de wa nai.

Not all Japanese are courteous.

Zenbu is correct in this sentence, but *min(n)a* probably sounds a little more natural, as in

2. 日本人がみ (ん) な (or 日本人み (ん) なが) 礼儀正しいわけではない。

Nihonjin ga mi(n)na (or Nihonjin no mi(n)na ga) reigitadashii wake de wa nai.

Not all Japanese are courteous.

In other words, *zenbu* goes better with inanimate objects while *mi(n)na* can refer equally to animate beings or inanimate objects. In 3 below, for example, *zenbu* is definitely odd, while *minna* sounds perfectly all right.

3.   A: ご家族はお元気ですか。
      Gokazoku wa ogenki desu ka.
      Is your family doing well?
      B: おかげさまで、み（ん）な（＊全部）元気です。
      Okagesamade, min(n)a (*zenbu) genki desu.
      They're all doing well, thanks.

With inanimate objects, either *zenbu* or *mi(n)na* will do, as in

4.   漢字を全部／み（ん）な覚えるなんて不可能だ。
      Kanji o zenbu/mi(n)na oboeru nante fukanoo da.
      It's impossible to learn all kanji.

ZUTTO ずっと all through; by far

Zutto has two main uses. First, it signals an uninterrupted state or period of time, as in

1.   十二の時から、ずっと英語を勉強しています。
      Juuni no toki kara, zutto Eigo o benkyoo-shite-imasu.
      I've been studying English (without stopping) ever since I was twelve.

Second, it is used to compare two things with a large degree of difference.

2.   アメリカは、日本よりずっと大きい。
      Amerika wa, Nihon yori zutto ookii.
      America is a lot bigger than Japan.

Don't use *zutto,* however, when the difference is not in degree but in style or in kind. Use other adverbs such as *zuibun.*

3.   英語と日本語はずいぶん（＊ずっと）違う。
      Eigo to Nihongo wa zuibun (*zutto) chigau.
      English and Japanese are a lot different.

BIBLIOGRAPHY

Alfonso, Anthony. *Japanese Language Patterns,* I & II. Tokyo: Sophia University, 1966.

Backhouse, A.E. *The Japanese Language: An Introduction.* Melbourne: Oxford University Press, 1993.

Hirose, Masayoshi, and Shoji, Kakuko, eds. *Effective Japanese Usage Guide (Nihongo Tsukaiwake Jiten).* Tokyo: Kodansha, 1994.

Makino, Seiichi, and Tsutsui, Michio. *A Dictionary of Basic Japanese Grammar.* Tokyo: the Japan Times, 1986.

———. *A Dictionary of Intermediate Japanese Grammar.* Tokyo: the Japan Times, 1995.

Miura, Akira. *Japanese Words and Their Uses.* Tokyo: Charles E. Tuttle, 1983.

Miura, Akira, and McGloin, Naomi H. *Goi* (Vocabulary). Tokyo: Aratake Shuppan, 1988.

Morita, Yoshiyuki. *Kiso Nihongo* (Basic Japanese), I, II, III. Tokyo: Kadokawa Shoten, 1977, 80, 84.

Nakamura, Akira. *Sensu Aru Nihongohyoogen no Tame ni* (For Sensible Japanese Expressions). Tokyo: Chuokoronsha, 1994

Petersen, Mark. *Zoku Nihonjin no Eigo* (English of the Japanese). Tokyo: Iwanami Shoten, 1990.

Shogakkan, ed. *Tsukaikata no Wakaru Ruigo-Reikaijiten* (A Dictionary of Synonyms with Explanatory Examples). Tokyo: Shogakkan, 1994.

Tokugawa, Munemasa, and Miyajima, Tatsuo, eds. *Ruigigo Jiten* (A Dictionary of Synonyms). Tokyo: Tokyodo, 1962.

Index